Long Live Salvation by Works

Long Live Salvation by Works

A Humanist Manifesto

Harry T. Cook

POLEBRIDGE PRESS
Salem, Oregon

Copyright © 2012 by Harry T. Cook

All rights reserved. Printed in the United States of America. No part of this book may be used or reproduced in any manner whatsoever without written permission except in the case of brief quotations embodied in critical articles and reviews. For information address Polebridge Press, Willamette University, 900 State Street, Salem, OR 97301.

The cover quotation is from The Society for Humanistic Judaism. Used by permission.

Interior design by Robaire Ream

Library of Congress Cataloging-in-Publication Data
Cook, Harry T., 1939-
  Long live salvation by works : a humanist manifesto / Harry T. Cook.
     p. cm.
  Includes bibliographical references (p.   ) and index.
  ISBN 978-1-59815-034-6 (alk. paper)
 1. Good works (Theology) 2. Salvation--Christianity. I. Title.
  BT773.C66 2012
  230--dc23

2012003478

To my Father and Mother,

Harry Theodore Cook & Bessie Alice Cameron
(1902–1977) (1917–1953)

who taught me to think for myself.

Cogito, ergo sum.

René Descartes
1596–1650

*Ah! — What a divine religion might be found out
if charity were really made the principle of it
instead of faith.*

Percy Bysshe Shelley
1792–1822

Table of Contents

Preface ix

Introduction 1

1 Faith and Works 5

2 Salvation 13

3 The General Situation 21

4 Whence and Whither Belief? 31

5 The Origins of Religion 39

6 Religions' 'Sacred' Texts 49

7 Misuse of 'Sacred' Texts 65

8 Reclaiming Our Secular Humanist Origins 75

9 Religion as a Search for Meaning 85

10 A Nontheistic Ethic of Restraint and a Commitment
to Inquiry 99

11 The Humanist's Goal Is Becoming Human 109

12 Negotiating Life as a Humanist 127

13 Practical Considerations 131

14 A Sermon for Would-Be Humanists 135

Epilogue 141

Appendix
Religion and Democracy: An American Experiment . . 147

Bibliography 159

Glossary 163

Index 165

Preface

The wording that constitutes the first half of this book's title came to me in an e-mail from a friend and fellow writer, Jack Lessenberry, a distinguished newspaper columnist and public radio commentator. He was praising an online essay of mine, which concerned what else religious communities might think of doing beyond preserving their fading identity as centers of rigid, not to mention immaterial, theological doctrine. The second half of the title had been lying in wait for many years among my voluminous collection of notes, sermons, lectures, and unpublished articles. Mr. Lessenberry's apt phraseology was the spark to the tinder.

The dedicatees of this book—my parents—took great care to expose their children to the religious principles and practices of Protestant Christianity, although my father had been reared in the Catholic Church. He departed from that fellowship precisely because its hierarchy took a dim view of people, especially Catholic people, thinking for themselves.

In fact, it was Msgr. Charles Coughlin, the radio priest of the 1930s, who was the precipitant force that drove my father away from the church of his youth and young adulthood—a church that my Scots mother with Presbyterian and Methodist background would have been happy to join had it meant that much to her husband. It did not, and thus did I end up attending a series of three Protestant Sunday schools: first an Episcopal Church then two more Methodist churches. In the first I began to learn by rote a young child's version of the catechism, thinking even then what a worthless exercise it was, even though I was told that doing so promised great rewards having to do with ice cream at the end of the year.

It was from Methodist nuns—all of them married women of a certain age—that I learned about the Bible and its contents. With one exception among them, I was never taught what to believe, but only what to learn. And learn I did, becoming, even in my gauche boyhood and even more gauche adolescence, entirely familiar with the Bible—though at an appropriately superficial level. I grew up listening to the sermons of Methodist ministers in the late 1940s and '50s. Apart from their annual Commitment Sunday rants against the consumption of alcoholic beverages, they sometimes preached about social concerns and civic morality. The one male Sunday school teacher I had was a physician who during the years of his internship in a New York City hospital had been nurtured on the liberal, left-leaning sermons of the late Harry Emerson Fosdick. Dr. Rodger's topical-in-nature Sunday school lessons were concerned with how the individual might attain usefulness in adult society. When at long last I entered a graduate school of theology, my father sent me a letter to which, uncharacteristically, he added a postscript referring me to a verse of scripture: "James 2:17." I had to look it up, and you should, too, because it is the biblical cornerstone for the structure and substance of this book.

I am much obliged to Lawrence E. Alexander, Publisher at the Polebridge Press, for his willingness to risk yet another book-making project with me, and to Tom Hall, that doughty New Englander who, with grace and no end of patience, suffers the prolix nature of my prose and then makes it readable.

Harry T. Cook

Introduction

Christianity has been plagued by doctrinal conflicts from its beginnings, even while *in utero*. The cultural context in which it struggled into life was itself a battlefield of ideas, concepts, and increasingly hardened positions. Here and there in the New Testament gospels are to be found references to two of the several opposing forces in first-century CE Palestinian Judaism: the Pharisees and the Sadducees. The former were innovators who had adopted for guidance in belief and practice a good deal of Judaic literature other than Torah; the latter, having accepted Torah as the sole controlling document, were primarily concerned with the ritual and sacrificial apparatus of the Temple.

The evangelists generally seem to have held both groups in contempt, using them as foils in narratives that held them up to ridicule. Think here of the miserable sinner of a toll collector who ends up in the inner court of the Temple at the same time as a Pharisee. The self-acknowledged sinner goes down to his house justified, while even for all his prayers the self-important and preening Pharisee suffers the storyteller's scorn.

Beyond that rivalry were other parties, including those we today would call terrorists, whose members interpreted for themselves the beliefs and practices of the then-regnant Judaism and used such interpretation as inspiration and excuse for such outrageous behavior as civic disruption, execution-style killings, and assassinations. The so-called *sicarii*, or "men of the dagger," were a by-any-means-necessary outfit, among whose chief aims was ridding their homeland of foreign invaders. The dagger-men were the shock troops of the Jewish-Roman wars. You could compare them to al-Qaeda or the Taliban in our own time.

It was in such a context that the early sayings of the various and often contradictory Jesus figures of the synoptic gospels (Mark, Matthew, and Luke) and of the Gospel of Thomas[1] appeared. Because those sayings were no doubt transmitted and massaged in oral traditions, and eventually set down in what were probably competing documents, no one can now be sure of whose version of the Jesus figure said what.

In any event, those sayings—mostly reflecting the ethical wisdom genre—seem to have served as the founding statement(s) of what I choose to call "Jesus Judaism" or "proto-Christianity." I hypothesize further that first-century CE Palestinian communities largely of the peasant or common laborer class were drawn to the countercultural wisdom of those sayings[2]—in a way similar to how the peasant/laborer classes of the mid-twentieth century in India were drawn to the ethical wisdom of Gandhi—and emerged as a distinct faction of Judaism, one that no doubt soon aroused powerful resentment among the Pharisees and Sadducees and other established parties. This may well account for why these groups came to be depicted in the gospels as enemies of Jesus. And since the earliest gospel narratives made their appearances at least 35 years after the execution of the Jesus figures they portray, it is no surprise that these groups saw Jesus Judaism as the enemy.[3]

If it is a fact that such "sayings communities" had come to an appreciation of the ethical nature of their religious commitment and therefore looked less to the cultic demands of Judaism, perhaps it was those of this more liberal orientation to whom the author of the Epistle of James was speaking when he wrote that "faith,[4] ... if it has no works, is dead."

Notes

1. A document notably influenced by Gnosticism that was found in 1945 in a cave near Nag Hammadi, Egypt. It is a Coptic translation of a much earlier Greek document and is thought to have been buried in the fourth century. This writer joins a number of New Testament scholars in hypothesizing that its provenance is early first-century. On this point, see Pagels, *Beyond Belief*, 30–75.
2. See Cook, *Seven Sayings of Jesus*, 13–49.
3. Matthew 10:17: "Beware of them ... they will flog you in their synagogues."
Mark 13:9: "You will be beaten in synagogues."
Luke 21:12: "They will hand you over to synagogues and prisons."
John 16:2: "They will put you out of the synagogues."
4. Faith, in that context, meant the content of belief.

CHAPTER 1

Faith and Works

Paul's utterances regarding faith and works are summed up in Galatians 2:16: "We have come to believe in the Anointed One, Jesus, so that we may be seen as right by trusting in that One, and not by doing the works of the law, because no one will be seen as right by the doing works of the law."[1] An unknown writer, writing in the spirit of Paul and who gave us the Epistle to the Ephesians, streamlined the idea thus: "For by grace have you been saved through faith, and this is not your own doing; it is the gift of God—not the result of works, so that no one may boast."[2]

The authors of a recent new translation of what are widely considered to be Paul's authentic epistles[3] demonstrate that key terms in the apostle's work have been sometimes deliberately rendered according to theological agenda. They say Paul's rhetorical tone and syntax was deliberately altered to suit an evangelical fundamentalist initiative. For example, the Greek phrase *ek pisteos christou*, usually translated "faith in Christ (Jesus)," really means "trust of Jesus," i.e. his wisdom and teaching. *Pistis* and its derivatives have commonly been rendered in English translations as "faith."

This new translation and consequent understanding, if accepted as valid, would have a profound effect on contemporary analysis of Augustine's and Luther's use of Pauline theology where the concept of "faith" is concerned.

Augustine, a fourth-century CE African bishop—who, by the way, did not know Greek—would have read Ephesians 2:8a as "*Gratia enim estis salvati per fidem.*" *Fidem*, being the accusative of *fides*, means "faith." Generally "faith" refers to the deposit of belief as well as to its more active sense of "believing in"—as in *Credo in unum deum*.

If the author-translators of the aforementioned book are correct, the preceding creedal statement would be correctly rendered as "I trust in one god." And the author of the Epistle of James would have said, "Trust without works is dead." Ronald Reagan was only too happy to reach both entente and détente with the Soviet Union over arms control, but his mantra was "Trust but verify." What verifies trust is the visible, palpable work that proceeds from it. James would observe: "You say you trust, then show me the proof. That's how I know you trust"—meaning that the action performed on the basis of trust is what matters; otherwise trust by itself is Paul's "hollow gong or crashing cymbal." One's trust that something is the right or moral thing to do is the motivator of the work.

For Augustine *fides* was by definition the precursor to belief and belief to knowledge: "If you are not able to know, [then] believe [in order] that you may know. Faith precedes; the intellect follows."[4] *Fides* comes to a human being, Augustine says, by the irresistible grace or gift of God: "He (God) goes before the willing that he may not will in vain."[5] Therefore, anything by way of works or any other human action unconnected to that grace-provided faith would be beside the point. If Augustine had understood *fides* as "trust," it would be an entirely different story. The scientist in these latter days trusts that his inductive method of research is sound, and after repeated testing can see and believe that his hypothesis has held up. The "work" that proceeds from it will vindicate the trust.

Martin Luther clearly saw that *fides*—in his native tongue, *glauben*—was likewise a divine gift. For him, faith obtained one's salvation from very real eternal damnations before which Luther quaked in fear. He took to heart the Ephesians passage and was wont to proclaim *sola fides* as well as *sola scriptura*. Here is what Luther had to say about faith and works:

> Faith is the work of God within us, which changes us and gives us new birth from God.... Faith cannot help but do good works all the time. It does not stop to ask if good works ought to be done, but before anyone inquires, it has done them already and continues to do them without stopping. Anyone who does not do good works in this manner is one who does not believe.... Therefore, it is impossible to separate faith and works as it is to separate heat and light from fire.[6]

Now suppose someone takes Luther at his word and agrees with his understanding, yet cannot discover in himself an impulse to believe that Luther's God and Luther's Christ have anything whatsoever to do with him. Such a nonbeliever would have to conclude that nothing he does, however clearly it appears to be a good work, is in fact any such thing.

This conundrum illustrates the difficulty of connecting actions that are obviously altruistic in spirit and in truth to the necessity of religious belief. It is such a conundrum that excited the late Christopher Hitchens and animates Sam Harris and Daniel C. Dennett, the professional atheists of our time. Speaking for millions of people who may not share their sharp-edged critique of any form of religious faith, each in his own way insists that morality need have no grounding in any religion or religious impulse whatsoever. I shall not footnote their books here; they are readily available and their authors' points of view well-known.

The point in mentioning them is that each makes a persuasive argument against the necessity of basing a moral theory on any theistic belief system. None of them would even raise the question of faith versus works, but would simply survey the catalog of what reasonable persons would term "good works" and agree that they were such.

Thus the faith versus works tension is totally theological in nature. If one believes that the Bible ranks somewhere between a valid governing document and the inerrant word of an omnipotent and omniscient deity, then the will of that deity must be absolute. It was such a belief that drove Luther to his utterly Teutonic idea that even a person's "faith" had to be entirely of divine initiative, and any "work" that did proceed from it proceeded not because of, but as often as not in spite of, the individual performing it. Luther's view was that unless a work proceeds from faith it cannot avail salvation from the natural punishment that human beings deserve for sin—that is, for their chronic separation from God. In fact, he held that works by themselves avail nothing—a contradiction of the canonical Epistle of James.

Here's how Luther dealt with that:

> I do not hold it to be of apostolic authorship, for the following reasons: Firstly, because, in direct opposition to St. Paul and all the rest of the Bible, it ascribes justification to works, and declares that Abraham was justified by his works when he offered up his son. St. Paul, on the contrary, in Romans 4[:3], teaches that Abraham was justified without works, by his faith alone, the proof being in Genesis 15[:6], which was before he sacrificed his son. Although it would be possible to 'save' the epistle by a gloss giving a correct explanation of justification here ascribed to works, it is impossible to deny that it does refer to Moses' word in Genesis 15 (which speaks not

of Abraham's works but of his faith, just as Paul makes plain in Romans 4) to Abraham's works. This defect proves that the epistle is not of apostolic provenance....[7]

At this point the person of reason and reality closes the door. First of all, no one knows who was and who was not an "apostle" in the historical sense of the word; second of all, there is no clear consensus on what it may have meant at any particular time to have been known as an "apostle." Insisting that the provenance of James is not "apostolic" does not diminish the value of its understanding of the relationship between belief and deeds.

And so in this matter, at least, the thinking person would cast his or her lot with Hitchens and company. It is not the doing of a good work that matters. It is the attempt to do it and the consequence of having done it. If I dash into traffic to pull an elderly person out of harm's way and sure death, my action is not so much the point as the fact that the elderly person goes home alive and uninjured.

Luther's descendants can argue that it was my "faith" in God the Father, God the Son, and God the Holy Spirit that was the impetus for my action. But what made it a good work (besides my reaffirmation of the worth of moral behavior) was the consequence that the elderly person was unharmed, that those who loved and cared for him or her were not grieved, that an insurance company did not have to pay a hospital bill or the family a funeral bill, or that a driver was spared personal anguish and possible criminal or civil charges.

The consequence or intended consequence of any act makes it either good or bad.

Assume that I, an agnostic, secular humanist, were to feel impelled to save the elderly person from death or injury. I would have been moved to do so with neither any thought to the commandment of a transcendent power nor any impulse to pursue an external ideal. I would have done so because I would want another to rescue me under similar circumstances. I would have done so because a human being alive and unhurt, when he or she can be both, is always a better proposition than one dead or injured.

Indirectly quoting George Santayana, Richard Rorty wrote that "the only source of moral ideals is the human imagination.... Most of Western philosophy is, like Christian theology, an attempt to get in touch with something larger than ourselves."[8] Rorty advocated the cessation of metaphysical questioning about the source of ideals or morals as well as whether one's choices to do this or that can be ascertained to have been correct in a theoretical sense. Rather, he proposed, the human impulse to care in concrete ways is the source, and the consequence validates its having been acted upon.

With that in mind, consider again the term "faith." It is used in a variety of ways, seldom intended to convey the idea of "trust." When one says he or she has "faith" in another, it generally means that he or she "believes" or "hopes" that the person in question will not treat him or her badly. Saying one has "faith" in God generally means the same thing, that is, that the deity of the person's imagination will somehow be the protector or the rescuer or the intervener to save whatever it is that needs salvation. In fact, "faith" is usually a major hedge against a possible and undesirable outcome. It is "hope" with a pious tinge.

What if the word "courage" were used in place of the word "faith"? A person faced with any one of "the thousand natural shocks that flesh is heir to"[9] might (1) acknowledge its reality, (2) face its potential threat to health and happiness, (3) plan non-passive and realistic ways to deal with it, (4) actually act in a sane way to mitigate its effect and affect, or (5) accept the results of one's best efforts so to do. That is the definition of courage. The "trust" factor comes in thus:

> Where is my strength? My strength is in me; my strength is in me and in you and in you.[10]

Maybe it is the "trust and try" rather than the "faith and works" couplet that is at issue. One can fall to his knees in petitionary prayer and beg an unseen deity to remove a cup from one's lips, or one can seize the chalice and drink from it, thus testing its power.

A "work" that proceeds from such "trust" will have its source in the person who performs it because it was obvious that it needed performing. That source will include the person's upbringing and the values with which he or she has been imbued. Therefore, one could not reasonably have expected, say, a thoroughly indoctrinated Hitler youth to perform altruistic acts without a considerable rehabilitation of his appreciation of what it means to be human.

In any event, a work performed because the performer believes an external power or ideal mandates it falls into the same category of one performed because Der Führer has ordered it or the ideology expects it. The knowledge of the correctness of a work performed out of belief that an external force has urged or mandated it will always elude one who is driven to ask if it was, in fact, the correct thing to do. Unless one resorts to imagining inner voices, a human representative of an external power or ideal (guru, lama, priest, rabbi, minister) will always serve as the appellate tribunal, and hence an action's correctness would perforce be dependent on a human judgment. As the pioneering humanist rabbi Sherwin Wine asked rhetorically, "Where is my strength?" His answer, "My strength is in me and in you... and in you."

Notes

1. Author's translation and paraphrase.
2. *Ephesians* 2:8–9 NRSV.
3. Dewey, Hoover, McGaughy, and Schmidt, *The Authentic Letters of Paul*, 2010.
4. *Sermo*, 118:1.
5. *Enchiridion*, 32.
6. Luther, "An Introduction to St. Paul's Letter to the Romans," 124–25.
7. *Luther's Works*, vol. 35, 395.
8. Rorty, *An Ethics for Today*, 2011, 8–9.
9. *Shakespeare*, Hamlet, Act III.1.62–63.
10. Lyrics to a song by Rabbi Sherwin T. Wine (1928–2007).

CHAPTER 2

Salvation

"Being saved" in one way or another by one agency or another appears to have been the classic desideratum in Western religions, certainly in Judaism and Christianity. For the former, it began with the self-serving myth that Yahweh delivered the people Israel from indentured servitude in Egypt and for their trouble awarded them a promised land. Because little or no evidence of an exodus exists, a crucial question arises: From what did Israel need to be saved? An answer emerges from history in the re-inhabiting of Canaan when Cyrus of Persia conquered Babylon and freed the Judeans and Israelites. The answer was obvious: from political, social, and economic exile.

Despite the tone poem known as Isaiah 45, which identifies Cyrus as God's messiah and credits Yahweh with his benevolent disposition toward Israel, it is a stretch even to consider that a Persian monarch was employed by the imagined deity of a small population to effect its freedom from exile. Textual evidence cited by James B. Pritchard[1] suggests that Cyrus's beneficence was as calculated as it was graceful—that his restoration of sacred sites to various minorities among his consolidated empire of Persia, Babylon, Sumer, and Akkad was a way of forestalling small-time but nettlesome rebellions.

Cyrus's decree, celebrated in Isaiah 45 and certainly alluded to in Isaiah 40, enabled the establishment of a Hebrew state in Palestine in the time of Ezra and Nehemiah (midfifth century BCE) together with the rebuilding of the cultic site and, possibly, the walls of Jerusalem. And for maybe a century until the post-Alexandrine age of the Seleucid and Ptolemaic rivalry, Cyrus' will was done. The eastern coast and immediate interior areas of the Mediterranean constituted the arena in which that rivalry was played out until Rome took over ca. 63 BCE. Judeans in particular bore the brunt of the struggle, often as pawns in a larger battle. The Book of Daniel sheds a *Gone With the Wind* kind of light on that era.

By then it was no longer Babylon's Nebuchadrezzar[2] or the warring Seleucids and Ptolemies, but the Romans from whom the Jews sought deliverance. And into that geopolitical maelstrom descended the generation we meet in the texts of the gospels. For the most part, they were long-suffering peasants whose limited destinies become further circumscribed by events entirely beyond their control—such as Herod Antipas' rebuilding of Sepphoris and the construction of Tiberias, both of which demanded that resources be channeled and labor conscripted.

It was during that era that the public careers of Jesus of Nazareth and John the Baptist have been depicted as having begun, suggesting that they came to prominence in their opposition to the treatment of the peasant class.[3] Any "salvation" for such people would had to have come from a realization—forced or otherwise—on the part of Herod Antipas and his court that they could not get away with treating people like cattle. The Baptist's remedy was to predict the end of the world, telling people to shuck off material concerns while at the same time "repenting"— that is, changing their minds and hearts about what was truly important. The Nazarene's advice to people of his economic class was to seek the kind of social and political regime they desired "within" or "among" themselves and to press on as best they could.

Off to the right of both the Baptist and the Nazarene was a group sometimes called the "Zealots," but more accurately the aforementioned *sicarii*, or "men of the dagger." They were basically contract killers whose targets were those perceived by zealotry as Roman functionaries or sympathizers. The zealots were not above committing atrocities against Jews to force them into rebellion. An oft-repeated story has it that the *sicarii* destroyed Jerusalem's food supply so that the Jews would have to resist the Roman siege without the option of suing for peace.

All of these strategies—the Baptist's, the Nazarene's and those of the *sicarii*—were means to the end of "salvation." None of them worked. The Baptist was parted from his head. The Nazarene was apparently swept up in a Roman fever to crucify all known opponents. The *sicarii*, some of whom held out until the bitter end at Masada, perished. What salvation?

The word "salvation" in the Judeo-Christian stream of thought originated with the root ישע, which means something like "enlarged," or "spacious" as opposed to cramped, crowded and constrained. A verb form would go to the static idea of "preservation" and the dynamic idea of "deliverance." A related Hebrew word means "to redeem," as in paying a ransom or price for a cherished entity or person. The former conveys the idea of a space, the latter the action of some agency. The parable of the prodigal son depicts him as ending up through his own disastrous choices constrained and economically cramped. When he arrives home, he finds a capacious welcome and an enlargement of his life. This aptly illustrates the idea.

In Christian literature, "salvation" reflects the Greek σωτηρία and its verb form σώζω, "to save," conveying the idea of being healed or made whole. It may be from this concept that Christian theology came to see salvation as restoration to a former state. If one takes at face value the story of Adam and Eve and its variations in other mythologies, the concept of salvation will seem closer to the idea of redemption or healing. Conversely, understanding the linear nature of history suggests that salvation by any name may repeatedly occur or not occur in the ebb and flow of events.

Returning for a moment to the rescue of the elderly person walking into traffic, it may be that he is likely to make such an error whenever he takes a walk. Sometimes he escapes unharmed due to light vehicular traffic or the caution displayed by motorists. On the one celebrated occasion, he is saved by an alert passerby. He is not restored to a former state but maintained uninjured in the same state. Or if he were to have been run down and whisked off to the hospital for surgery and treatment, he might be restored to some semblance of wholeness—in which case both his immediate rescuer and the surgeons and their assistants in the hospital will have been agents of his "salvation." But it will be only an interim salvation, because he will eventually die—if not as the result of another traffic mishap, then from some ailment or another, or by simply wearing out. No passerby is able to care or risk enough to forestall that.

The fact is that the only life we know has beginnings and endings, and in one way or another each and all of them are natural. Among human beings life arises through a merging of sexual gametes, and by one agency or another it ends in death. So one who is a saved from death, as was our hypothetical elderly peripatetic, lives only to die another day. It cannot be avoided. If a nation or people is delivered from the dread hands of one tyrant, it may be that in another generation or two they will be seeking yet another saving intervention. One may be saved from death on the road only to be killed in a house fire. There is no ultimate salvation from dying and death.

Enter the Apostle Paul and the gospel myth makers of the late first century CE, and salvation becomes a state of being that extends beyond life itself. "So shall we ever be with the Lord," said Paul in 1 Thessalonians 4:17. And the path to this salvation is through belief: "For since we believe that Jesus died and rose again, even so, through Jesus, God will bring with him those who have died." A more familiar variation on the theme is alluded to by those John 3:16 banners at the Super Bowl: "For God so loved the world that he gave his only begotten son that everyone who believes in him may not perish but have everlasting life."

Before the impatient reader turns the page, the author can offer a soupçon of salvation: The words "everlasting life" (in the Greek of the text ζωην αἰώνιον) do not necessarily or even probably refer to the length or perpetuation of life so much as to its immediate depth and breadth. Both reason and experience support the conviction that the Jesus revealed in the ethical wisdom attributed to him[4] can give meaningful depth and breadth to a life whatever its length, provided said conviction serves as a general rule for one's actions.

Thus "faith" or "trust" or "belief" can be a secondary agent of "salvation," but the primary agent is the one doing the "faithing" or the "trusting" or the "believing." The operative Greek New Testament words here are πίστις (faith, belief, trust, confidence), πιστός (to be trusted or believed, or of persons "trusty, loyal") and πιστόω (to make trustworthy or believable). It is this latter word (a verb) that applies to the search for salvation. A person looks about and discovers any number of alternative ethical programs among moral philosophies or codes of conduct or understandings of human worth. At some point, his reasoned experience adopts one such, and he lives his life according to its principles. It may result in his possession of ζωην αἰώνιον—a depth and breadth of existence that makes the days of his years, however long, fulfilling for him and for those whose lives his touches.

To reprise Rabbi Wine: Where is this one's light? Where is his hope? Where is his strength? It is in him and in those like him. Salvation is a state for the here and now because any there and then is beyond human ken—neither beyond imagination, perhaps, nor beyond possibility, but beyond knowledge.

So to the well-meaning Christian fundamentalist who asks, "Are you saved?" one can return the not unkind answer, "From what, pray tell? Or from whom?" The reply will be something like "eternal death" or "the evil one." The response can be: "I will die eventually, and from everything I know about material existence, I will be dead forever even as my physical remains return first in physical form, then in chemical form to the biosphere. As for an 'evil one,' I am doing battle with more than one of them already in the form of political, social, and economic tyrannies that dehumanize and destroy."

Such answers will not avail for our fundamentalist interlocutor, but that's as it may be. Because my light is in me . . . and in you.

That said, how does the nonbeliever, the agnostic secular humanist, hope and work for salvation? And from what and for what?

The ethic of Jesus of Nazareth seems to have been founded on the oft-quoted maxim of Hillel the Great: "What you hate, do not to do to another." At the basis of such wisdom is the conviction that the dignity of every human being must be respected first, last, and always. And when one behaves in an undignified, antisocial manner, he must be called to account, not hated. As for the tyrannies mentioned, one can do battle with them in the same way Mohandas Gandhi and Martin Luther King, Jr., did—after the manner and teaching of the Nazarene with passive resistance against violence and passive insistence that power must hear truth spoken to it and act accordingly.

Salvation need not be conceived of as hope that one will survive life through resurrection or immortality, but rather as the conviction that one can make a difference in the time and place when and where one lives—and perhaps be remembered by his or her children and grandchildren and even great-grandchildren for having done so. Not, of course, that such remembrance is the point.

Salvation can be a matter of using and getting other people to use the resources of the planet we share with the rest of Earth's biota—including the air we all breathe, the water we all drink and the light by which we live—in ways that respect their nonhuman provenance and with the understanding that some resources are finite.

Long live salvation by works.

Notes

1. Pritchard, *Ancient Near Eastern Texts*, 316.
2. Although popularly known as "Nebuchadnezzar," Nebuchadrezzar is the preferred spelling. See *The Interpreter's Dictionary of the Bible*.
3. Crossan, *The Historical Jesus*, 207–64.
4. Matthew 5:39/Luke 6:29.
   Matthew 5:41.
   Matthew 5:44/Luke 6:27.
   Matthew 18:22/Luke 17:4: "Forgive as often as it takes" (author's translation).
   Matthew 7:12/Luke 6:31: "Treat others as you would be treated" (author's translation).

CHAPTER 3

The General Situation

Evidence suggests that the common sentiment has begun to swing back toward an appreciation of the world as sacred. Until recently, of course, it had been increasingly seen as secular—that is, for what it actually is: a material reality governed by physical laws, in the process of becoming better understood by observation and rational analysis, and in thrall to no deity of human invention or imagination. The emergence of modern science, the Enlightenment, and the Industrial Revolution would have been impossible without a tilt toward secularism and a compartmentalization of religion.

An unintended result of the Reformation was to put God and religion in their place, still both relevant to humanity but less essential. The Lutheran revolution demonstrated that after 1,500 years, the Catholic Church no longer possessed a monopoly on truth. The response of Mother Church was not an accommodation to the realities of the free market but a reaction characterized by the rigidity of form and function prescribed by the Council of Trent.[1] Trent was the first initiative specifically crafted to combat modernism and was succeeded in that effort by Pius IX's First Vatican Council of 1869–1870, which established the infallibility of the pope speaking *ex cathedra*.

Although they spurred a revival of religious observance, the novel horrors of World Wars I and II, notably including the Holocaust, constituted a setback for conventional theism. I remember interviewing Elie Wiesel when he came to Michigan in the late 1980s and directly asking him how his Holocaust experience had affected his religious belief. "God and I have not been friends for quite some time," he said. "God and Auschwitz—one cannot say those two words in the same sentence."

It may be that the relatively recent impetus for the swing back towards sacralism, at least politically and socially, came with the issuance of the 1973 U.S. Supreme Court decision famously known as *Roe v. Wade*, in which a majority of the justices held that abortion of human life in the womb was to a certain extent a private matter between a woman and her physicians, and about which morality could not and should not be legislated. The reaction was delayed because former President Lyndon Johnson died the day the opinion was handed down (January 22, 1973), and for a week or so the news media dwelt on that event. In due course, though, the antiabortion movement mobilized in protest, engaging along the way what turned out to be a formidable ally: an array of Christian evangelicals who were already seriously annoyed by the Internal Revenue Service's stripping of Bob Jones University's tax-exempt status on the grounds of racial discrimination.

Evangelicals seemed at first to accept *Roe v. Wade*. W. A. Criswell, former president of the Southern Baptist Convention, was unequivocal: "I have always felt that it was only after a child was born and had a life separate from its mother that it became an individual person." W. Barry Garrett in the Baptist Press of January 31, 1973, opined that "religious liberty, human equality and justice are advanced by the Supreme Court abortion decision." Nevertheless, that decision became the rallying point for evangelicals who had soured on Jimmy Carter and were eventually to be welcomed into the ranks of the Reaganites.

Ever since their embarrassment over the 1925 show trial of John Scopes[2] for teaching evolution in a Dayton, Tennessee, high school, evangelicals had been shelling their peas quietly in the moonlight; but as it turns out, they bore an enormous and simmering resentment against the civil rights and antiwar movements of the 1960s as well as the leftward thrust of Christianity propelled by the new intellectual freedom that issued from the Second Vatican Council and the parallel rise of bible scholars and philosopher-theologians who would no longer allow their work to be limited by sectarian or denominational necessities.

The explosion of a new kind of Roman Catholicism featured nuns out of habit running soup kitchens and homeless shelters, priests saying mass in English in settings resembling coffeehouses, and longhaired guitar players keening rock-like religious music. And all this, coupled with the so-called Death of God movement advanced by some of the aforementioned scholars and theologians, sluiced right handily into the stream of thought and emotion produced by a younger generation impatient with racism, militarism, and the conventions of the 1950s. That collective upsetting of the applecart was symbolized in a bizarre way by Woodstock and its "if-it-feels-good-do-it" sentiment and ably urged on by the vernacular mass, by priests and nuns leaving their orders to marry, by Protestant preachers taking up in earnest the historical-critical approach to figuring out what the Bible really might be saying. And all of that ran full force into the soldiers of evangelical fundamentalism marching as to war.

Some of their generals—Pat Robertson, Jerry Falwell, and Bill Bright (this last, of the Campus Crusade for Christ)—did not hide their unhappiness over what was the effective defeat of the United States by the Viet Cong and what it seemed to mean: namely, that America might no longer be perceived as having a divinely assigned manifest destiny. So intertwined was their belief system with their national chauvinism that men like these found such a thought anathema. Moreover, the challenge that Rosa Parks, Martin Luther King, Jr., and Malcolm X had brought to white America deeply disturbed those who had counted on things to remain largely as they were. The uproar of Watergate set off by the suspicion that Richard Nixon had been hounded from office by the very enemies on his list shook the foundations of civic certitude and virtue.

Those who made their homes there were tired of being told they lived in "the Bible Belt"—as if such an address were undesirable. They were tired of being marginalized. A reaction was in the making. Enter in 1976, Jimmy Carter, a true son of the South, Annapolis honors graduate, submarine commander, peanut farmer and Bible-believing Baptist. His campaign made no bones about the latter, and the nation was scratching its head over its first avowed "born-again" president. For a moment in time, the evangelical movement thought they finally had their man. But he consulted with Jesse Jackson and whined about a "national malaise" for which the electorate might well be blamed. He allegedly mismanaged the Iran crisis that erupted in the siege of the Teheran embassy and the infamous 444 days of hostage captivity. Those evangelicals who had given Carter some slack and had adopted a wait-and-see attitude toward his presidency abandoned him and marched *en masse* into the camp of Ronald Reagan, who talked one of the best religious games of any president since Abraham Lincoln.

Neither Lincoln nor Reagan was a churchgoer in his adult life. But Lincoln knew the Bible and its rich cadences, not to mention the ethical substance of its Hebrew prophets, a tradition he seemed to have internalized and was unashamed to employ in his governance and public utterances. Reagan used the cant of chummy, feel-good American Protestantism to give a religious aura to his most sentimental comments and speeches. In doing so, he rather mindlessly embraced the social agenda of the Right. That was good enough for the evangelicals, who not only became a force in the contemporary Republican Party but energized and gave voice to the many people for whom the ferment of the 1960s had made it a confusing and frustrating time. The payoff came when Reagan let it be known that he had consulted with Falwell before announcing the nomination of Sandra Day O'Connor to the Supreme Court. O'Connor's antiabortion *bona fides* had evidently been in question.

Reagan's successor, Bush I, was not disposed to be an errand boy for the Christian Right, not even for the political Far Right, and for that and other reasons became a single-term president, succeeded by one who also said he was a true believer but conducted his life and some of his governance like a true hypocrite. As a result of Bill and Hillary Clinton's 1993 vainglorious attempt to change the health care insurance climate in the United States, the far Right—of both politics and religion—set out to demonize them both. Even now, the radio rant-and-rave talk show hosts and their callers-in still speak darkly of Clintonian plots and intrigues, schemes now connected with the alleged stratagems of Barack Obama.

Of George W. Bush these same founts of wisdom and insight spoke mostly in hushed and reverential tones— except when they exhorted him to lean rightward or else. In so doing, such voices of the radio waves, of the Christian evangelical pulpit, and of the Far Right in Congress and statehouses (now more numerous than ever) are not embarrassed to proclaim that the United States is a

"Christian nation" and to applaud their favorite harridan, Ann Coulter, when, post-9/11, she declared generally of Muslim nations that "we should invade their countries, kill their leaders, and convert them to Christianity." For not only is this world the realm of the sacred and presided over by the god of the Christian bible, but America is that god's chosen instrument to restore the world to its Edenic splendor—beginning with cleaning up the mess that Democrats and New Dealers and religious heretics and hippies and journalists and devotees of *The New York Times* have made of the land of the free and the home of the brave.

Part of that purge can be seen in the alarming and disappointing retrogression of the Roman Catholic Church, which enjoyed a brief but bracing draught of fresh air through the windows John XXIII opened in his broad gesture of *aggiornamento*. For a quarter of a century, Karol Wojtyla, one of the most literate and worldly popes in living memory, was clearly bent on taking Catholicism and as much of the rest of the planet as he could manage back to a worldview that posits a deity just over the horizon of human apprehension—but "there," nonetheless, and watchful besides. That deity, it is said, handed down a will and a way, a set of laws and observances for humankind to obey, follow, and practice. The full and absolute truth of that will and way, of those laws and required observances, allegedly reposes in the accumulated, received wisdom of Catholicism that the pope and his minions conserve and from time to time pronounce from their Roman Olympus. Wojtyla's successor, the Austrian prelate, Joseph Ratzinger, has doubled down on that effort.

They have their counterparts in Islamic mosques, in the *shuls* of Orthodox Judaism, and in the pulpits of evangelical Protestantism. Such venues are the platforms of an uncompromising theism that posits an omniscient, omnipresent, and omnipotent deity who/which may be bargained with through the medium known as prayer. This deity is said to be responsible for the existence of all that is, with the possible exception of certain phenomena that theists denominate "evil"—the list thereof depending upon which brand of theist is doing the denominating. Again, depending on which group of theists is doing the claiming, the deity (called by various names of human invention) favors the way of the particularly claiming group and holds other ways in contempt. For Christian theists, the world is a sacred, deity-filled realm.

Having said as much, theists then divide into tribal priesthoods and parse their theisms as best suits their local, regional, or national necessities—the Tower of Babel *redivivus*. But it gets worse, because theists cannot always—or even usually—agree on the details, for which reason one set of monotheistic believers occasionally drives aircraft into the skyscrapers of another. It is why monotheistic imams and mullahs issue the *fatwa* against The Great Satan. And not incidentally, it is why some American Christian monotheists are still saying that 9/11 was the judgment of their posited deity on a nation that coddles homosexuals, tolerates abortion, and levies high taxes. Yes, high taxes. The tax question has become a big agendum of the Christian Right. I will leave it to political scientists in consultation with psychiatrists to figure out that one.

The sum of it all is that the waters of sacralism are lapping around our ankles on an incoming tide. How high the tide will reach is unclear, but it bids fair to rival that of the Noahic flood for changing the landscape. Far too many places on Planet Earth are ravaged by violent conflict, and virtually every incidence of it can be traced to competing sacral views. The relatively calm waters of American life have often been roiled by politicians and elected officials who are neither embarrassed nor hesitant to invoke the god of Christianity and the agenda of his (His?) disciples—and this in a nation that has long since discovered and avowed its pluralistic nature. It is a pluralism that includes adherents of nontheistic Asian religions, of Islam, of various stripes of Judaism, and plenty of agnostics. All too many of those who presently hold political and governmental power interpret the Freedom of Religion clause in the Constitution chiefly as one intended to protect what they insist was the religion of the Founding Fathers: Protestant Christianity. (To be sure, most of them are willing to include contemporary Catholicism either out of ecumenical concerns, to avoid alienating the in-laws, or because of its uncompromising antiabortion stance).

A more objective reading of the Freedom of Religion clause suggests that the government ought to stay out of all religious activities and refrain from any official endorsement, covert or otherwise, of any religious expression or point of view. A clearer reading of the amendment suggests that freedom *from* religion is guaranteed as well.

That is just about where America is near the beginning of the second decade of the so-called Third Millennium. Polls, for what they're worth, show that close to 80 percent of Americans say they "believe in God," and that some significant number of them claim to attend religious services regularly. Leaders of religious institutions wonder about that latter statistic, since many of them suffer rather gravely from empty-pew syndrome. What is clear is that denominationally unaffiliated churches, especially those known as mega-churches, which hew pretty closely to a conservative theological and social message, are more successful—if numbers are the measure of success here—than their mainstream counterparts. The educated guess is that churches or temples that traffic in uncomplicated certitude are better patronized than those that pose questions and entertain ambiguity, especially on what are commonly seen as "moral issues."

A title I once considered for this book was *Religion May Be the Death of Us All*. It certainly has been the death of many, and it always comes about in the name of some unseen god whose adherents are perfervid in their conviction of that god's reality and that god's word and will—beliefs that of course favor that god's adherents in some self-aggrandizing way. Meanwhile, as in politics and war, so it is in religion: Might makes right. But since there must be a better way, this is a good time to doubt—to doubt or to be willing to doubt that what one's clan, class, kith, or kin asserts by way of belief is—to use the late Richard Rorty's helpful characterization—any more than "contingent."[3] That would be one constructive way to rethink the place of religion in a secular world.

Notes

1. The Council of Trent was the 19th such ecumenical council of the Catholic Church. It was convened in several sessions between December 13, 1545, and December 4, 1563. Besides issuing condemnations of what it called "Protestant heresies," its promulgations came to define the life of the Roman Catholic Church for the next 500 years. The Second Vatican Council (the 21st ecumenical council) was called in 1962 by Pope John XXIII to modernize some aspects of the church's teachings and practices.

2. Scopes was chosen as the defendant by a precursor to the American Civil Liberties Union to contest the validity of a Tennessee statute prohibiting the teaching of evolutionary biology in a public school. He was defended by Clarence Darrow, and even though a jury found him guilty, his only penalty was a $100 fine. But such were the evangelical theatrics of the guest prosecutor, William Jennings Bryan, that the trial ended up resembling a freak show in a traveling circus.

3. Rorty, *Contingency, Irony, and Solidarity*.

CHAPTER

4

Whence and Whither Belief?

Part of what gives religion a bad name is the almost universal habit religious people have of turning the stuff of notion into the assertion of truth. It does not take much encouragement to get an evangelical Christian or Orthodox Jew, a practicing Catholic or devout Muslim to inform you of the truth about "god" and life. Each has his or her holy writ and creed, and is likely to know them well enough to quote portions of them to you. Each adherent will be a thoroughgoing theist who "believes in god" in the same way he or she believes that the sun will rise on the morrow and that night follows day. If you respond by saying that you have come to understand that the sun will rise tomorrow and that night will follow day, and that you have come to such understanding through the rationalization of observation, you may not get an argument.

The argument will come when you gently say that you do not "believe" those things but "know" them to the extent that they have so far proven to be so—and then say that you have, however, been unable to make any such observations with regard to a god, much less a rationalization of a nonobservation, and that therefore, you yourself do not have sufficient knowledge to say there is a "god," whatever that may mean. If pressed, you might go on to say further that you can make out no discernable will or law of a god the signs of whose presence or power or prerogative you have not observed. You might say that your mind is not closed to the possible knowledge of a god, that you would certainly entertain such an idea when testable data appear to make such an idea a reasonable proposition. You might go on to say that, for you, knowledge is attained when what has been learned has then been tested and found to be so, or to be real rather than ephemeral. You might say that you actually do trust the validity of some knowledge—for example, that human beings have vast intellectual and emotional potential, that they have created civilization and culture and art, that they have discovered the power of love and often genuinely care for one another, and that you therefore think that human beings at their best may offer an indication of where the evolution of the species may be heading. You would also want to concede that human beings often go one step forward and two back, that what Robert Burns called "man's inhumanity to man" is as present a reality as anything, and that our kind occasionally displays something dark and threatening and deeply disappointing, as if we were devolving rather than evolving.

The response of your theist friend is not likely to be printable. Like as not, it will be accompanied by a frustrated shake of the head, as if to indicate that you simply don't get it. He or she may say that you will be the object of many a prayer in order that you may come to see the light. You might thereupon say that you don't understand how this wish, however devoutly it invokes the mercies of a supposed deity, could affect you. But of course you would be honest and gracious enough to say that if light in any form were to dawn, you will certainly give careful consideration to what it reveals or illumines, and report back. That will be, effectively, the end of useful conversation on this subject between the two of you. To be sure, your friend may try other tactics to weaken your resolve, but you should refrain from responding in kind, because it is an axiom of human behavior that you cannot reason a person out of a position he did not reason himself into in the first place. However, a person who *did* reason himself into a position might be reasoned out of it and into another more reasonable position.

That is why a true a-theist is not someone who refuses *a priori* to give intellectual assent to the existence of a god. The true a-theist is exactly what the Greek-derived term means: "not a theist," that is, not a believer in an omnipotent, omniscient, omnipresent deity (hence the increasingly common term, "nontheist"). In matters metaphysical the true a-theist is agnostic—from *agnosis,* not-knowing or (having) no knowledge. The honest a-theist does not rule out the possibility that a god exists, it's just that he or she requires testable data. A helpful metaphor is to imagine a person standing under a street lamp. The street lamp provides a radius of light, illumining to one degree or another whatever is there to be illumined. That truth is the source of the hackneyed joke about the drunk who is looking under the streetlight for something he lost elsewhere. What would be the use of looking in the dark?

Using the metaphor of the street lamp, we might say that, in matters of religious sentiment, the line between knowledge and belief generally follows that fine interstice between the lamplight and the darkness beyond it. What one knows by observation and rational analysis is what one can apprehend in the light; that which one "believes on faith," must needs lie beyond the light's radius. It was once commonplace and commonsense to believe that Earth was flat. Why? Because that's pretty much what the ground at one's feet appeared to be. And the sun could be seen rising and setting at the edge of land or water. But over time human observation and reasoning got more sophisticated, and at last it could be understood that in fact Earth wasn't flat, which is to say that it has no edge from which one might fall headlong into the void. Isaac Newton would go on in his time to help us understand that not only was Earth not flat, but a certain force called "gravity" pulled all objects toward the unseen center of Earth and could be opposed only by the application of a contrary force, and then only for so long—in short, "what goes up must come down."

It remained for the technology of rocket propulsion and space travel to show that Earth's gravity can be overcome. Thus was the radius of the lamplight pushed farther out so that more and different phenomena could be observed and, over time, understood. That process increased and altered human comprehension at the same time that it exposed the mistakenness of some existing beliefs and replaced them with what could reasonably be called factual knowledge. And it *is* a process we are talking about here, this expanding of circle of the known—and one that according to all available evidence has limitless potential. The radius of the lamplight is not fixed; it is expandable; it can be pushed out as men and women of daring and determination vow to push it out, as they form hypotheses, test and retest them, and eventually restate them as theories like those that propose a heliocentric solar system, natural selection, and relativity. Some hypotheses, like that defining gravity, finally attain the exalted status of "law."

We have just described the transformation of belief into knowledge. It admittedly leaves a lot unsaid. It leaves unexamined the possibility of knowledge of "god" or of other unseen deities. Such knowledge at this stage of human intellectual development lies beyond the radius of the lamplight—how far beyond is a subject for speculation. The only agreement in the debate between you, the agnostic a-theist, and your theist friend may come when you concede that you have the possibility, however remote, of knowing whatever he or she "believes." If the radius of the lamplight could ever be widened sufficiently to find reliable data enabling the rational observer to say, "Aha, there is god," then you and the theist would have come to common ground. Your theist friend is not likely to buy that proposition, because he knows and you know that such knowledge is, to quote the Hebrew psalmist, "too wonderful" (Psalm 139:5)—too good, in fact, to be true.

Thus it is that all theistic religion is based on belief rather than knowledge. And if one chooses to live by belief rather than knowledge, he or she chooses a potentially dangerous way. The difficulties arise when believers try to pass off the content of their belief as sure knowledge that everyone should affirm lest they be in some way less than acceptable. The indefatigable attempts of the Christian Right to mandate the teaching of "creationism" or "intelligent design" alongside or even instead of tested theories in public school science classes constitute a perfect example of this. If one takes the most benevolent view of the creationists' initiative, one must concede that it is based on deeply held belief. A more cynical view of the same efforts might see them as part of some hidden political agenda. Either way, if education is supposed to deal in knowledge and the search for knowledge, creationism—which is at best a thinly veiled theology and a purveying of belief—has no place in any serious educational institution, public or private. Yet a reasonable interpretation of the Freedom of Religion clause certainly provides for creationism to be taught with impunity in nonpublic schools. It does not, however, permit the same for public schools, because the clause clearly prohibits anything that would tend to "establish" by the hand of government a particular religion or any of its tenets.

This is not a brief against belief. It is a brief against belief being imposed as knowledge. And that is the besetting problem of contemporary religion. If a person invests his belief with the conviction that it is knowledge, anything is possible. Or if one bases his or her choices and decisions on some supposedly holy writ that is parsed by a supposedly infallible priesthood, once again anything is possible. It is possible to interpret many an entry in any religion's scripture as warrant for war and death. Passages here and there in the Hebrew Bible and Holy Qur'an seem to invite just such warrant. The relatively moderate amount of time and energy it would take to apply the historical-critical method of interpretation to any such text would soon enough disclose that they are not of divine provenance but of human origin. Their validity for the present time would then have to be judged against the evolving ethic of human civilization. The Holocaust, for example, taught much of Western Civilization that genocide could no longer be tolerated, no matter what some ancient and revered text might seem to say. Belief in the acceptability or validity of a text, tradition, or concept cannot be an adequate justification for any action that injures or kills another human being, or violates his or her personal dignity. That is the human-centered ethic that has been evolved in recent centuries. It is what gave birth to the idea and the reality of the United Nations. No belief or belief system that goes against that ethic is to be tolerated.

So what is to be done about this business of "belief"? Well, we must first take a hard look at the phenomena that likely constitute the origins of religion and therefore of belief, then at what is called "scripture," and finally at what will have to happen to enable Western civilization to reclaim its secular origins. Then we will be ready to contemplate and entertain a new role for religion as a secular humanist discipline. And this we must do, for only thus can religion embrace and complement the arts and sciences as venues and vehicles for the advancement of the human race beyond the problematic place it occupies today — a chancy way station on the evolutionary journey from savagery to fully developed humanity.

CHAPTER 5

The Origins of Religion

Who knows where it was on the evolutionary path? But somewhere a member of *Homo sapiens* or one of his immediate predecessors paused in the midst of some kind of daily activity to wonder whether forces he couldn't see or hear or touch or taste or smell could be responsible for whatever it was he was up against or having good luck with. And what was it that might have occasioned that novel thought or impulse? One much-considered surmise is that the phenomenon of the death of parents or tribal elders at some point began to impinge upon what in this later developmental stage of being human we would call the emotions. Some human being or proto-human being shed the first tear attributable to deep feeling, and it might well have been the death of an older relative that gave rise to the feeling.

Even as smitten as our society is by the cult of youth, we know that the passing of elders from the scene leaves a kind of void. We see that the works and accomplishments of the dead live after them, sometimes for quite a while, and once in a while for good. Nevertheless it is a shocking thing to contemplate that Bach or Mozart or Michelangelo or Rembrandt—or one's own father or mother—could have been what each was, and produced what each produced, and yet end up in the same state of decay and decomposition as any other animal matter.

So may have begun the denial that what was dead was really dead. Soon came the reverence of the immediate dead, and eventually that of longer-dead ancestors, whose humanity was gradually effaced by a growing veneration of what they were recalled to have been and eventually made out by their descendants to have become. It was not too giant a step from there to declaring them "divine"—that is, dead but alive, not-present but present, and certainly possessed of sufficient power to effect and affect the living and their world. Somehow out all of that must have come the beginnings of morality—a kind of "if-I-do-this-then-that-will-happen" impulse, or the hunch that consequences may have causes that go beyond the obvious: "Does my little plot of land get flooded every rainy season because that's how it is, or do I get wiped out because I have done something wrong, have failed to communicate with and appease my ancestors through the tribal rituals?" Where cause-and-effect is sufficiently obscure as to be considered a mystery that is not only beyond knowledge but beyond the ability to know it, the door is opened for the positing of unseen, purposive forces and their eventual personification—a process that has apparently been replicated many times over the human millennia.

Communion with the dead/divine became associated with propitiation, which often enough involved the ritual offering of human beings who were considered expendable to the tribe—among them children or sexually ripe young women who were deemed surplus for the purposes of propagation. The Elohist, whose text dating to about 750 BCE forms a recognizable portion of the Pentateuch, upped the ante to make the only son of a mythical patriarch the subject of divinely mandated sacrifice (see Genesis 22), but then undertook a backhanded condemnation of human sacrifice through the *deus ex machina* of the ram in the thicket. Some 250 years earlier, in the Yahwist myth of Cain and Abel, sacrifice to the desert god had been reduced to animal flesh (Abel) and agricultural products (Cain). Yahweh, interestingly enough, is depicted as not yet appreciative of vegetable sacrifice. It didn't have to be human, but it had to be animal—hence the divine approbation of Abel and, alas, his murder by his rejected vegetarian brother.

It remained for some of the Greek mystery religions to associate communion with the deities by eating and drinking food that was said, in effect, to be or to represent their flesh and blood. If that sounds familiar, it's because that is the model along the lines of which the Christian eucharistic liturgy was developed, so that by the time of the Counter-Reformation the formula *Accipite, comedite, hoc est corpus meum* (take, eat, this is my body) was understood literally. By the time religion had gotten around to that, the concept of the transcendent-but-immanent deity was firmly fixed across ethnic and cultural lines, at least in the Western world.

Anthropologists and evolutionary biologists have frequently commented on their observance of animal dominance behavior, how that in a given situation the prey will avert its eyes from the predator, will lower its head, and even prostrate itself. Rangers in Glacier National Park in Montana prescribe that very behavior for those unavoidable instances in which the human being meets the grizzly on the latter's turf and must, as it were, beg for his or her life. Thus in their solemn bows, liturgical prostration, hushed tones, humble petitions, and the commonly prescribed posture of prayer—kneeling, with eyes closed and head bowed—human beings seem to have adapted animal dominance behavior to their habits of religious ritual. As power was consolidated in tribal circumstances, leaders began to demand of their subjects similar acts of appeasement. And it is not surprising that in some cultures such leaders—often called "kings"—were commonly considered members of a superhuman master race. Can it be that *Homo sapiens* has been aping his animal cousins, or is the predilection to such behavior part of our genetic makeup?

Another approach to the origins of religion leads us in quite a different direction. Some portions of the archeological record point to the likelihood that the forebears of the people who eventually came to be called "Israelites" migrated from the coastal cities of the eastern Mediterranean around 1300–1200 BCE, presumably to escape the depredations of predatory economic oligarchies. They found their way into the hill country of what is now northern Israel and became subsistence farmers who, according to recent analyses of the archeological data, seem to have reacted to the class oppression they had escaped by forming exceptionally nonhierarchical, nonaggressive egalitarian communities. And in these communities, there seems to have gradually evolved what some scholars think may be some of the case law—"If A, then B"—that appears in Exodus and in revised form in Deuteronomy. The emphasis had apparently been on how members of a migrant community now operating outside of former social and economic constraints could best get along. Thus may have arisen the rather humanist ethical system that evolved to become part of the utterances of the biblical prophets with whom the Jesuses of the synoptic gospels and the Gospel of Thomas seem to have been acquainted.

In due course—one supposes that the egalitarianism of the communities eroded as natural human competition for power and position arose—the source of their body of evolved law was less and less attributed to their own organization and more and more to an unseen desert god sometimes known as "Yahweh." It seems reasonable to consider that community leaders of the second and subsequent generations found it increasingly difficult to make their governance stick, and therefore adopted as a legitimizing force the god of peoples indigenous to the region, those whom their predecessors had encountered in the process of their migration from the coastal cities. The Sinai myth eventually transformed what had been an inductive, from-the-grassroots-up evolution of the law into a deductive from-the-top-down imposition. It turned a movement into an institution that needed an unseen deity and an intermediary priesthood to maintain authority and control.

Yet another proposition about the origins of religion has to do with the dawn of the agricultural age following the recession of the ice cap somewhere around twelve thousand years ago. Anthropological analysis of the archeological record has suggested that identifiable religious cults arose among human communities at about the time they were making the transition from being hunter-gatherers to tillers of the soil. In a tribal culture, hunter-gatherers appear to have operated on a kind of lone-wolf basis. An agricultural economy was more communal and necessarily entailed division and classification of labor. Someone got to "sit in the office" and oversee the operation while others had to go into the field in the heat of the day and do the hardscrabble work. That was about the time organized religions appeared, and they may well have become the venue for control in the economy.[1] An elite class, whether by might or right conferred, arose from tribal elders who appropriated divine authority for their position and the demands made on those not in authority. A god or gods were cited as the source of and force behind the implementation of a do-it-or-else system that divided tribes into classes or castes, with the elite expecting, demanding, and receiving an often generous portion of the harvest of which they were neither sowers nor reapers.

The phenomena of nature have always been curiosities to *Homo sapiens* and must be considered as part of the origins of religion. Think of the immediate post-Ice Age human being standing on a promontory overlooking a vast sea on a moonless, cloudless night. He surveys the dark, mysterious vault above him stippled with countless points of light, some brighter than others, some larger than others. He knows he did not make what he sees. He knows he cannot control the changes he sees taking place above him as seasons come and go. The impenetrable mystery of the rising and falling sea at his feet unnerves him.

That same man while working his plot of land may be overtaken by a sudden storm of rain or wind, perhaps accompanied by what we know as lightning and its resultant thunder. He wonders aloud in some language or protolanguage why all that is occurring. He may see the effect and assign the cause to the rain or the wind. He knows he didn't cause all this tumult, but wonders what or who did. He may have held a frightened conversation on that matter with another tiller of the land like himself, and thus began human inquiry into the cosmos. It was inevitable that the first answers were largely what we would now call metaphysical guesses. And it is not difficult to see how that enterprise of inquiry soon got taken over by a priestly elite, who were probably perceived to have a higher knowledge of things—or presumed on their own that they should and therefore did have.

Nevertheless, what had gone on were observation and assemblage of data in some such manner as this: *The sky gets dark; the wind rises; water falls from above; frightening shafts of light flash; something makes a big noise; and my soil washes away, the seed with it.* Then came the uniquely human leap: *Why?* There was the beginning of philosophical and scientific inquiry. And it would take several millennia before the inquiry was wrested from the grasp of religious authorities by independent seekers whose reason led them to question the conclusions drawn in antiquity and imposed by religious authorities upon the masses.

Well into modernity, Copernicus, Galileo, and Isaac Newton began to publish the results of their observations and calculations, and the literate world was introduced to some new and very different understandings of how things were and worked. Newton, for all of his genius, was still looking for the hand of his church's theistic god behind or within the otherwise natural phenomena of which he had such a clear understanding. Writing in *Principia Mathematica,* Newton said: "If only we could derive... phenomena of nature from mechanical principles.... For many things lead me to have a suspicion that all phenomena may depend on certain forces by which the particles of bodies, by causes not yet known, either are impelled toward one another and cohere in regular figures, or are repelled from one another and recede."[2] When Newton said "certain forces," he meant, I think, "as yet unknown forces," and his confessed "suspicion" suggests that the god of his upbringing was fast becoming a word symbol for something he hoped would eventually make for a rational explanation of the cosmic mechanics he had so acutely observed.

In their own ways, Copernicus in the fifteenth and sixteenth centuries and Galileo in the sixteenth and seventeenth had shown conclusively that the immutable laws of Aristotle immutably cemented into the Catholic understanding of the cosmos were in error. Nothing but the moon revolved around the earth. Both, together with other observable bodies, revolved around the sun. Jupiter's moons and the sunspots observed by Galileo helped undermine what the church had long taken on the basis of scripture passages to be true about the cosmos. Then, roughly three hundred years after Galileo, along came Charles Darwin, who almost against his will concluded from observations made in the course of his epoch-making voyage on the Beagle that species evolve through the process of natural selection. Darwin's epoch-making work not only showed that the Genesis stories were either untrue or never meant to be taken as rational explanations, but also paved the way for the development of genetics and all the tools and insights that branch of science would bring to the human understanding of how things are.

Then, of course, Albert Einstein graced the twentieth century with his theories of relativity, which are based on two postulates: one being that the speed of light in a vacuum is constant and independent of its source or its observer, and the other that the mathematical forms of the laws of physics are invariant in inertial systems. That leads to the assertion of the equivalence of energy and mass and of change in mass, dimension, and time with increased velocity. An extension of that theory (called the General Theory of Relativity) includes gravitation and other acceleration phenomena. In ways that are only gradually becoming apparent, the relativity theories have knocked into the proverbial cocked hat most of the religion-based assertions about how things are.

Because the advance of science with its well-tested theories has seemed to many to contradict certain teachings of some religions, there arose in certain quarters the notion of an unbridgeable chasm between the two. One of the more melodramatic illustrations of that supposition was the infamous 1925 trial of high school biology teacher John Scopes in Dayton, Tennessee. Scopes' offense was that he had acquainted the youth of Dayton High School with the Theory of Natural Selection—what the religious yahoos of the time called "evil-lootion." The trial became a contest between reason and faith in the larger-than-life *dramatis personae* of Darrow and Bryan. Bryan immolated himself on the altar of biblical literalism—he himself providing the faggots and Darrow the flame. Memorable as it is, however, the Scopes trial does not provide a fair picture of the juxtaposition of religion and science. The practitioners of these two disciplines pose different questions about the same phenomena and seek different answers—thereby suggesting that what is called "scripture" and its contents are not to be confused with entries in the scientist's laboratory notebook.

Note

1. Charles C. Mann, writing in the June 2011 *National Geographic*, reports that a site in southern Turkey known as Göbekli Tepe was constructed ca. 9600 BCE by people who evidently experienced an urge to worship some kind of deity. Dozens of enormous stone pillars were brought to the site and assembled as a kind of temple over what must have been a span of years, requiring an organized food provision system that may have spurred the tilling of nearby land. If that hypothesis is borne out, it will be necessary to concede that religion preceded agriculture in the human epoch at least at Göbekli Tepe .

2. *Principia*, 382.

CHAPTER

6

Religions' 'Sacred' Texts

The Merriam-Webster Dictionary defines the word *scripture* as "a body of writings considered sacred or authoritative," noting the word's Latin etymology meaning "a product of writing." Scripture in the classic sense is like portraiture, a product of painting or photography; or like sculpture, a product of sculpting; or like architecture, a product of the design or planning for a structure or arrangement of objects; or, finally, like literature, a product of artists' ideas expressed in the writing of a particular language. Scripture, then, like portraiture or sculpture or literature, is the work of human beings.

One can view a portrait or a sculpture or an architect's edifice and say, "How inspired!" As I stood in the Galleria dell'Accademia in Florence for the first time and regarded Michelangelo's monumental *David*, I had what some would call a "religious experience." I knew I was seeing the work of a genius, of one who had attained an appreciation of the human form as few others ever had. *David*, like the *Pieta*, embodies a statement, an idea that hovers powerfully in the human mind—in cyberspace, as it were—and is of immeasurable value beyond the material of which it was hewn. If *David* should be destroyed tomorrow and ten thousand to-scale replicas made of it, its magnificence would endure for all time. The same is not true of all scripture, any more than it is of all sculpture or architecture or portraiture or literature. But just as it is true of some examples of each of those forms, it is indeed true of some scripture.

Some Christians are fond of saying that the Bible is "the Word of God." Never was there a statement emptier of meaning. No matter how it is parsed, it has no useful content outside sectarian conceit. Both of its nouns are highly metaphorical in nature and invite individual interpretations across so wide a spectrum as to render them all but useless in rational discussion. To be sure, the collection of documents and fragments of documents known as "the Bible" contains some critically important and sublime passages—texts that have taken on significance beyond their individual words in the life of Western civilization. But to say that is not to say that the Bible is the "Word of God"—it is only to say that portions of the collection are eminently worth paying attention to in a life that seeks depth and meaning.

Take, for example, the ten commandments so prized in the Christian tradition. They are, of course, part of a collection of some six hundred such mandates and directions that appear here and there in the Pentateuch. The story is that Moses received a specific number of commandments directly from Yahweh in the course of an encounter upon a mountain in the Sinai. The Charlton Heston movie has made that story credible to millions of people, and its veracity is pretty much insisted upon by some Orthodox Jews and millions of fundamentalist Christians across the world. It is, however, a thing of myth. It has all the earmarks of mythology—which is not to say the myth is unhelpful or devoid of truth, as long as it is understood as myth.

The relocation of the aforementioned migrants from the cities of the Mediterranean's eastern shore to the hill country of today's northern Israel in the thirteenth century

BCE and their development of case law probably provides a more credible proposal for how the bulk of Jewish law was arrived at: Elders of the tribe gathered around the communal fire figuring out how to make life work in dependable ways, how to maintain internal security so life could be productive and safe. It must have occurred to such leaders that by promoting an egalitarian sharing of the community's resources and proscribing covetousness, they would probably have a better chance of preventing theft, and thereby have a better chance of preventing violence and killing. Adultery and the risks that it entails would no doubt also have been important considerations. And if they could make it a requirement to honor the elders' or parents' traditions, they would have a better chance of making it all stick. But as insurance, perhaps, they decided to add the authority of an unseen god. The formula might well have been, "The desert god with whose blessing we seem to be at peace up here in the hills is desirous of a certain code of behavior. Here it is. Make it work."

Soon enough, it was the supposed existence of that god that captured the interest and the imagination of the people, rather than the practical demands of the law. Instead of following the wisdom of the law that evolved in their own community and out of the exigencies of that community, people sought to gain the favor of that god through the performance of rituals. Soon enough, an intermediary priesthood-like elite emerged to interpret and enforce the law through the vehicle of ritual. Eventually, the details of ritual—most of it sacrificial in nature—came to be governed by other laws or commandments that were, of course, proclaimed by the elite to have divine warrant.

That is how the Bible got to be "the Word of God." And what a temptation it became for religious leaders to parse and interpret those laws in ways that served their own interests by enforcing a class system that favored the elite over the masses. Thus was effaced the egalitarian nature of those expatriate communities in which it all started, and with it what was an early humanist appreciation of a communal code. Generations upon generations of Jews and Christians have suffered as a result. The idea that expressions in any human language can be vended as "the Word of God" is ludicrous on the face of it. The idea that such expressions are to be or could be taken as conveying some absolute truth is dangerous.

In a lecture entitled "Texts That Are Sacred, Texts That Are Not," found in his *Reporting the Universe*, the American novelist E. L. Doctorow observed that the scriptures of Judaism, Christianity, and Islam "were produced or revealed in those ages when stories were all people had—and when their invention was the word of God."[1] Doctorow quickly goes on to explain that they were "the Word of God" because the people who invented them said they were. But, he added,

> When Bacon and Galileo insisted on putting claims of knowledge to the test with observation and experiment, storytelling as the prime means of understanding the world was so reduced in authority that today it is only children who continue to believe that stories are, by the fact of their being told, true. Children and fundamentalists.[2]

Taking a cue from Doctorow, any proponent of any religion would do well to consider—if he or she hasn't already done so—that the texts that define and spell out his or her religion are (or are derived from) stories first told in an uncritical age when no clear lines existed between fact and fiction, and, further, that truth may be discovered as well by what we call fiction as by what we call fact. "The heavens declare the glory of God, and the firmament showeth his handiwork" (Psalm 19) is not a statement of fact scientifically arrived at. It is an example of sheer, wondrous poetry that proceeded from the awed and informed imagination of some ancient bard who intuited that the whole of what he saw ablaze in the night sky must somehow be greater than the sum of its parts. That psalm presaged in poetry Galileo's more prosaic, though no less profound *Siderius Nuncius* ("Starry Messenger") of 1610, which went beyond observation to calculation. Only the least imaginative person would ever quote Psalm 19 as a proof for the existence of a god, much less of that god's supposed creative achievements. "In the beginning gods[3] created the heavens and the earth" is as lyrical a statement as the arresting four-note motif of Beethoven's *Fifth Symphony* or of the opening bars of Samuel Barber's *Adagio for Strings*.

I am persuaded that whoever first uttered those words was moved by the same or a similar impulse as Beethoven or Barber—an impulse or urge to celebrate the presence of meaning in the world. But surely any musicologist who attempted to extrapolate a theory of creation or so-called religious or philosophical truth from the *Fifth Symphony* or *Adagio for Strings* would soon find himself out of the musicology business altogether, or at the very least see his work relegated to a file labeled "L" for lunatic. Why has not the same fate overtaken theologians of theistic religions who try (and amazingly succeed) in passing off the texts of their traditions as "sacred"—that is, of divine authorship and conveying direct and absolute truth?

Both the Bible and the Qur'an are diminished by the use religious authorities make of them. Both collections are part gold and part dross, but because of the all-or-nothing hermeneutic by which they are too generally and frequently approached, one can be forced to accept the dross as gold, so that a Levitical commandment that mandates certain liturgical functionaries not to round the corners of their beards, or another that prohibits the sexual employment of the male reproductive organ for any purpose other than penetration of its female counterpart are elevated to equal importance with such foundational texts as these:

> You shall not oppress a resident alien; you know the feelings of an alien, for you were aliens in the land of Egypt.
> What does Yahweh require of you but to do justice and to love mercy and to walk humbly. . . .
> Yahweh is my shepherd; therefore can I lack nothing.
> If I speak in the tongues of mortals and of angels, but have not love, I am a noisy gong or a clanging cymbal.[4]

Too many purveyors of religion find it impossible to acknowledge that the literature they possess includes material encompassing everything from profound wisdom and insight, to superannuated rules and regulations, to downright ludicrous notions. To make such an acknowledgement would, of course, require such purveyors further to acknowledge that their texts are of human provenance and therefore liable to error and obsolescence. Were such acknowledgements to be made in good faith, the rest of the world might quickly come to acknowledge that some of those texts are among the most sublime in all literature. From a purely ethical, humanist point of view, the parables of the Good Samaritan (Luke 10:29–37) and the Prodigal Son (Luke 15:11–32), both of which seem to have made their first appearances in Luke, are not in any literature surpassed for their excellence in disclosing what it is to be truly human. In fact, neither of those parables requires much interpretation. They need only to be applied in life. And it doesn't matter, by the way, whether or not they originated in the corpus of Jesus' teachings—most evidence suggests that they did not—because, unique among such word pictures, they stand on their own just as they are regardless of provenance.

In any rethinking of the place of religion in a secular world, the guardians of religious texts will have to release them to the rigors of public discussion, therein to be plumbed for their wisdom and criticized for their vacuity. As one whose entire adult life has been an immersion in biblical texts, and as one who is an unabashed left-brained rational agnostic, I feel it eminently safe to say that the Bible, once pried from the death-grip of fundamentalism, will be able to more than hold its own as an important document of human civilization and development, and will attain the exalted reputation it deserves as one of the most monumental libraries produced in the human epoch.

The scene is a rare-book room annex at a well-known repository for documents of antiquity. The present author is a graduate student come on a field trip. He joins others in a dimly lit subterranean vault around the three sides of which are deep shelves from floor to ceiling, lined with ochre-colored drain tiles. Out of the ends of the tiles can be seen the somewhat tattered and ragged ends of what are obviously manuscripts of some antiquity. The professor-guide, with a sweeping, roundhouse gesture says, "Gentlemen, this is the Bible!"

Of course, the Bible is not, was not, and never had been a uniformly composed, edited, and printed volume with a beginning, a middle, and an ending—though common practice over the centuries since Gutenberg has rendered it as such. In fact, the German noun *bibliothek,* whence the English "bible," means library. All libraries have collections that vary from the sublime to the merely prosaic—from reprints of the *Iliad* to auto mechanic manuals. This is not to say that in every situation the former would be more important than the latter. It is to say that in any collection there will be a variety of literary types, and they will be of differing quality and relevance to different people in different times and situations. An application of that rubric to the Bible will quickly demonstrate that much of its varied textual content will prove itself helpful and relevant to those who seek wisdom for and meaning in life.

So if the Bible is not "the Word of God"—that is, of divine provenance—then what is it? If Qur'an is not the product of Allah whispering in Muhammad's ear, what is it? Demonstrably, these several texts are the work of exceptionally gifted and imaginative human beings whose visions of the world and human life were uncommon, memorable, and memorably articulated. Some of the texts are stories of the kind Doctorow described—stories that were key to the psychic survival of people, critical to their self-understanding and ethical development. As such, they are priceless relics that can, if properly and appropriately received by twenty-first-century people, inform, correct, and help shape choices and decisions.

Amidst the present activity of archaeologists working in Israel is a major deconstruction of the myth of a mighty Judea-Jerusalem monarchical complex ca. 1000 BCE. In light of that, one is compelled to take another look at the story of David found in 2 Samuel—David, the cinematic and quite possibly mythic war hero of that era; David, the sexual predator, who was depicted as being willing to have a brave and loyal soldier killed in a misbegotten effort to cover his own indiscretion. While the story may not be a report of one specific occurrence, it is certainly an account of how sexual irresponsibility based on selfishness and exploitation can and often enough does ruin lives. As such, the story is universal in import and application.

The two irreconcilable narratives of Jesus' birth and infancy that were crafted by the writers/editors of Matthew and Luke have often been embraced by certain Christians as further "proof" that Jesus was more than human. If received uncritically and without note of nuance, they would seem to say that. Indeed, one of the four fundamentals of fundamentalism is "the virgin birth of Christ." And for fundamentalists, that fundamental admits neither of rationalization nor of ambiguity. It means what it says. Such a simplistic hermeneutic, though, robs the stories of their mythological profundity, not to mention their particular historical significance.

Obviously composed either from a common set of source materials or, in part, from separately evolved ones, the Matthean and Lukan narratives are wondrously imaginative in trying to account for the significance of the origins of Jesus of Nazareth, the singular hero of the gospels. By the time these narratives were written—or at least made their appearance—the Jesus variously depicted in the gospels would have been dead for more than half a century. The religio-political situation of Jesus' world (ca. 4 BCE–35 CE) had been radically altered by the events of 70 CE—the destruction of Jerusalem, together with the Temple and its sacrificial apparatus. Synagogue Judaism and Jesus Judaism were on a collision course, and only one of them would be left in a dominant role. Much, therefore, was at stake in the necessary reconstruction of the Jesus story. (Remember Doctorow!)

If Jesus was not to be depicted as a proto-rabbi in what would become the emerging synagogue tradition, then as what or whom? The religious marketplace of the late first century CE featured a number of figures to whom various degrees of divinity were attributed, and it was to and for that marketplace the gospelers were gospelling. While the ethical wisdom attributed to Jesus was certainly revolutionary in its own way,[5] it was no competition for warring, dying, and rising sons of the gods. Therefore, the conservation and transmission of that ethical wisdom required the creation of a myth to compete successfully with other myths.

If New Testament scholar John Dominic Crossan is correct in his identification of Jesus as a wandering sage in the Cynic tradition, it must have been clear to the leaders and exponents of Jesus Judaism that such an image could not carry the day. So to answer the question that inevitably had to have been posed by prospective recruits ("So who was this Jesus, anyway?"), the compilers of Matthew and Luke took the opportunity to make a contemporary case for the divine origins of the one whose ethical wisdom they wished to advance. It may have been Matthew who first got the idea of appropriating and proof-texting Isaiah 7:14 ("Behold, a young woman of marriageable age shall conceive, and be delivered of a son..."). And perhaps he deliberately took the Septuagint's mistaken rendition of the Hebrew *almah* (young woman) into the Greek *parthenos* (sexually unspoiled girl) so as to convey a miraculous beginning of Jesus' life. At any rate, he thus made the gigantic leap from the child envisioned by an eighth-century BCE writer to a Nazarene youth said to have been born almost a millennium later.

Any competent practitioner of literary studies would quickly point out such a connection and praise it—not for its historic accuracy, for that would be impossible, but for its cleverness in making what the writers/editors of

Matthew saw as a vital point in attempting to persuade late first-century synagogue Jews to become part of the Jesus movement. That is, of course, a far cry from using the texts in question to "prove" some kind of supernatural origin for Jesus. The gospeler known as John skipped the quasi-biological material and went straight to the nomenclature of Greek philosophy in claiming by indirection that Jesus was the *logos* of God. That in itself should put the other "origin" texts in perspective.

Having once gotten straightened out in the matter of the birth and infancy narratives, one can more easily come to understand the passages devoted to the alleged "miracles" of Jesus—that is, the numerous healings and other episodes that require the suspension of reason and the acceptance of supernatural interventions. Twenty-first-century persons will naturally look at the healing of the blind or deaf person, the cleansing of the leper or the raising of Lazarus through their own contemporary lens, and recognize that those stories (again, remember Doctorow) were confected in the first century, when the understanding of sickness and death, as yet unrefined by the progress of scientific and medical knowledge, was far different from our own. The colloquy in John 9 about whether the man born blind was so afflicted for his own sin or that of his parents is typical of how such handicaps and suffering were understood.

It was in that context that the gospelers wove the miracle stories, perhaps from the skeins of oral tradition that had built up in the half-century since Jesus' time. It is necessary to put those texts in the same category as the birth and infancy narratives—that is, literary devices created (or appropriated and edited) for the purpose of giving heft to the image of the historic personage around whom Jesus Judaism was being built. This is not to deny categorically that Jesus may have enjoyed some extraordinary power deriving from his inner self. Gospel accounts frequently mention that those who encountered him declared that he had *exousia*—roughly translatable as an inner dynamic that distinguishes a person in memorable and effective ways.

Here I am reminded of an actual late twentieth-century event involving a man thought by the physicians of an eminent teaching hospital to be dying. A chance visit to the supposed deathbed by a humanist rabbi long since self-proclaimed as an atheist so invigorated the man that he was able to leave the hospital on his own two legs—and thereafter lived happily for many years.[6] No explanation has ever been given for what happened. But *something* happened, and those who witnessed it—themselves humanist and atheists—attribute it to the magisterial authority of the rabbi. In other words, we do not need to look beyond the human factor when trying to appreciate those things for which there is no ready explanation.

That brings us to the canonical texts concerning Jesus' supposed resurrection from the dead. The very fact that the one text that appears to be a totally bizarre and incredible "eyewitness" account (Gospel of Peter 10:38–42) is excluded from the canon suggests that the framers of the canon were dubious about such an event actually having occurred, and were thus more comfortable with texts that left the issue wreathed in ambiguity. The so-called "empty tomb" narratives in the synoptic gospels (Mark 16:1–8, Matthew 28:1–10 and Luke 24:1–11) have in each case women coming to the burial-place, in Mark and Luke to anoint the body for permanent burial and in Matthew "to see the sepulcher." Only in the Matthean version do any of the women "see" Jesus and run to tell unnamed disciples of the empty tomb. In Mark, the women tell no one anything "because they were afraid," and in Luke, the women are rebuffed by "apostles" who dismiss them as hopelessly hysterical.

It remained for Luke in the matchless "road to Emmaus" story and John in four of what are generally termed "post-resurrection appearances" to give some substance to story. But in each case, the texts offer fairly obvious clues that they are not to be taken as journalistic accounts of events. In the Emmaus story, Jesus suddenly appears to Cleopas and an unnamed friend, but they recognize the identity of their mysterious fellow traveler only when he breaks bread with them at the evening meal and then disappears into thin air. Beyond the obvious *deus ex machina* features of Jesus' coming and going is the unmistakable allusion to an early Christian eucharistic meal with an explication of scripture preceding a time of eating in fellowship.

Moving on to similar texts in John, Mary of Magdala is depicted as weeping at the entrance to an empty tomb, saddened that the corpse of the one she called "Lord" has been removed. Behind her was one she supposed was the custodian of the cemetery. She did not recognize him as Jesus until he spoke her name. It is reasonable to consider that the name-speaking is the key to understanding that text. Later that day, another *deus ex machina* is deployed as Jesus suddenly appears in a room even though the door is locked and unopened. The same occurrence happens a week later, and finally, in what seems to be a postscript from another "John," we find an episode in which Simon Peter recognizes the figure on the beach only when it has told the disciples, now unsuccessful nighttime fishermen, where to cast their nets—which lo and behold come up overflowing.

Consider another clue that "resurrection" is not about the reanimation of dead tissue denoting divinity of the raised one, but rather, perhaps, about seeking and finding meaning in indelible memory. This paragraph was written on an anniversary of the March on Washington in August 28, 1963, with the now-famous grainy shots of the late Dr. Martin Luther King, Jr., delivering his monumental "I Have A Dream" speech on television. As I watched the footage and heard that familiar voice intone those familiar words, I was "there" again, and it was "then." King was once more present to me, and all my youthful aspirations were rekindled. That does not make Dr. King physically alive again. And as powerful and as riveting and as dead-on-center as his words were, they do not make him divine. They do make him extraordinarily human and one of the significant figures in the human epoch. That is the sure thing that can be said of what are otherwise known as "sacred" texts. They are of human provenance, and their validity is to be determined by their usefulness and relevance in a given time by those who would take them seriously. In rethinking the place of religion in a secular society, this is a rule that will have to be always and everywhere in force.

To close this part of the discussion, I think it useful to allude to the much-touted originalist interpretation of the U.S. Constitution. As of this writing, it is a cause held dear by interest groups in America whose members insist that the 1787 document means now what it meant then and that each and every clause in it must be ultimately determinative of present law and policy. These groups know not what they say, and obviously cannot appreciate the social, political, and economic chaos that would ensue in the wake of such an interpretation. They are political fundamentalists in the same way that other groups are biblical fundamentalists in their belief, absent any factual basis, that every verse of every one of the sixty-six documents included between the faux-leather covers of their Bibles is the direct and final word of the deity they worship.

No less a patriot than Benjamin Franklin cautioned his fellow delegates to the Constitutional Convention even then poised to vote for the passage of the seven articles of the nation's founding document: "For having lived long, I have experienced many instances of being obliged by better information, or fuller consideration, to change opinions even on important subjects, which I once thought right, but found to be otherwise."[7] Franklin, like many of his colleagues in that momentous effort, had serious doubts about some of the provisions in the Constitution. He thought the document neither infallible nor perfect.

No text of human provenance—and commonsense tells us that all texts are of that provenance—is infallible or perfect. That goes for anything in the literature of any religion.

Notes

1. Doctorow, "Texts That Are Sacred," 53–54.
2. Doctorow, "Texts That Are Sacred," 54.
3. The plural "gods" is used because the Hebrew word used in the text (*elohim*) is plural: "gods."
4. Exodus 22:21 (author's translation); Micah 6:6–8 (author's translation); Psalm 23 (author's translation); and 1 Corinthians 13:1 (NRSV).
5. Matthew 5:39/Luke 6:29: "Turn the other cheek."
    Matthew 5:41: "Walk the second mile."
    Matthew 5:40/Luke 6:29: "Give up your one shirt as well as your one coat."
    Matthew 5:44/Luke 6:27: "Love your enemy."
    Matthew 7:12/Luke 6:31: "Treat others as you wish to be
    treated" (all author's translation and paraphrase).
6. This story has been repeatedly told by members of the late rabbi's congregation and confirmed by him. He was Sherwin T. Wine (see chap. 1 p. 11 and chap. 2 p. 18). The congregation was and is the Birmingham Temple in Farmington Hills, MI. Two members who confirmed the story are Harriet Maza and Marilyn Rowens.
7. Remarks written by Franklin but read by James Wilson before the Constitutional Convention on September 17, 1787, just prior to a vote of the delegates to approve the seven articles of the U.S. Constitution.

CHAPTER

7

Misuse of 'Sacred' Texts

One of the great blots on the image of Christianity is anti-Semitism. It is impossible to talk about anti-Semitism without acknowledging that its primary source was a branch of first-century CE Judaism that would later be known ideologically as "Christianity" and institutionally as "the church." I have spent the past four decades engaged in ongoing research and analysis of those texts gathered into what is commonly (if inaccurately) called the New Testament, and also the so-called patristic texts. Translation and analysis of those texts have demonstrated to my satisfaction that anti-Semitism had its beginnings in the historical developments that produced certain of these texts, and that such texts shaped attitudes and encouraged prejudices—all under the banner of orthodoxy.

First-century Judeans and Samaritans lived under economic oppression, to be sure, and that oppression had plenty to do with the colonialist expansion of the Roman Empire. The last stand at Masada, which by some lights was a culmination (if not quite the end) of the Jewish-Roman wars, was and is an indication of how much the religious tenacity of the Jews had been trouble for Roman occupation, even as it had for the Seleucids some 150 years earlier. According to Dr. Cesare Colafemmina,[1] documents indicate that the Emperor Titus forcibly relocated perhaps as many as five thousand Judeans to an area about 180 miles southeast of Rome now known as Venosa shortly after the siege and destruction of the Second Temple in 70 CE. Their deportation was typical of conquering powers in that time, and rather than exemplifying what we today would call anti-Semitism, it may reflect a general Roman disregard for non-Romans who happened to have been in the way. However, such drastic removal was of a piece with anti-Semitism from the late first century CE on into the Constantinian era. Meanwhile, back in Judea, an unforeseen series of events was afoot.

An itinerant wisdom teacher whom later first-century literature would call "Yeshuah" and an apocalyptic preacher whom that same literature would call "Yohannays" had apparently developed roughly contemporary followings that may for a while have been competitive. Some textual evidence suggests that the former may at first have been a follower of the latter. Both seemed to have appealed to the resentment of economic dislocations visited upon the populations of Judea and the Lower Galilee by an urbanizing Roman government of occupation. Both offended authorities—Yohannays, one of the Herods; Yeshuah, a Sadducee establishment and perhaps also the Roman proconsul in Judea. Yohannays was known for his "end-of-the-world" approach to justice, Yeshuah for his less aggressive, ethical wisdom approach. Evidently both were executed for being flies in the ointment: Yohannays first, Yeshuah not long after. Around both of them arose traditions, and for reasons that remain unclear, that of Yeshuah won the day—or thus is history construed in and by most of the surviving texts from that period.

It is my working hypothesis that a collection of ethical wisdom sayings attributed (correctly or not) to Yeshuah sustained a community of his followers for a couple of decades—roughly from 35 to 70 CE. Such sayings may have included the riff on Hillel for which Yeshuah gets more credit that he deserves: "Do to others as you would have done to yourself."[2]

From the vantage of my hypothesis, I see that what I call the communities of "Yeshuah Judaism" were formed around those sayings, much as earlier communities of Israelites and Judeans formed around the injunctions of the Torah. In fact, I suspect that the Yeshuah sayings were deliberately edited, arranged, and cast in the way they appear, for instance, in Matthew—that is, so that they would remind people of similarly arranged Torah passages. Matthew 5:1–2 illustrates these points: "When Yeshuah saw the crowds, he went up the mountain, ... and he began to speak, saying: How happy like the kings are the wretched, for theirs is the rule of heaven; how happy are like the kings those who are sad, for they will find strength..."; and so on. That portion of Matthew continues as a series of sayings attributed to Yeshuah—again, edited and arranged to make it appear that he had said them all at once in one place to one audience, when it is more likely that the editor of Matthew, who was doing his compiling around 85 to 90 CE, gleaned the material from several sayings sources.

In some circles in different times, Matthew 5, 6, and 7 was known as the "new Torah." So already Yeshuah Judaism was cutting the umbilical cord. The author/editor of Matthew went on to show his true colors when he distorted a passage from an already existing document that told of Judeans going about seeking "testimony" that might get Yeshuah in trouble with the authorities. Matthew took it and unaccountably added the adjective "false," so that Judeans (often referred to as "Jews") are depicted as seeking "false testimony" against Yeshuah. It is an early but clear case of what would become known as "anti-Semitism."

Clear textual evidence in another later first-century or early second-century document known as John reveals a growing and nasty split between "synagogue Judaism" and "Yeshuah Judaism." In a contrived narrative about Yeshuah encountering a Samaritan woman at a tribal well, Yeshuah is made to announce that worship in Jerusalem is outmoded. Now true followers will worship "in spirit and in truth." Mark and Luke—which, like Matthew, seem to have appeared in the last third of the first century—variously depict Yeshuah's detractors as "scribes" or "Pharisees" or "Sadducees"—in other words, as various factions of Judaism with which Yeshuah Judaism was seen to be in competition.

But so complete by then was the severance between the two movements that in John, Yeshuah's detractors become "enemies" and are called (with a clear curl of the lip) "the Jews." Part of what may have been going on is that the emerging movement was trying to tell its story using a vehicle already present in the cafeteria of religious image and language modeled on Greek mystery religions—in particular, those that are replete with dying and rising sons of gods. Yeshuah, being human, eventually died. It remained for the person or persons responsible for Mark, the first thing of its kind, to tell a story about the execution of Yeshuah, in which he is depicted as a martyr. Mark appeared shortly after the destruction of the Temple in 70 CE, perhaps in response to that event.

Yeshuah Judaism may have been somewhat estranged from Temple tradition, but this estrangement could be characterized as that of an adolescent from his or her family as part of growing up and becoming independent. It seems clear that the destruction of the Temple was a colossal blow to Jews of every stripe and in every place. Yeshuah Judaism, in particular, was left with little if anything on which to hang its hat. The collected wisdom sayings of Yeshuah could no longer sustain the community now deprived of that against which it was rebelling.

So Saul of Tarsus and later a Yeshuah Jew called John who seemed quite smitten with Hellenism began separately and as many as fifty years apart to invent a story along the lines of a Greek mystery religion, a myth in which Yeshuah begins to be called *ho christos*—Greek for "the anointed one" or "messiah." The abyss now yawns. Yeshuah Judaism was evolving beyond its roots and tradition and was being morphed into something new—new and, its exponents insisted, better. The formula found often in Matthew was, *You have heard it said of old, but I say to you.* Saul of Tarsus in his new incarnation as "Paul," was saying that living under the law—under Torah—is living in darkness. One must now live by the freeing *charism* of faith.

Anyone who reads the Christian gospels sees quickly that most of the blame for the supposed lynching of Yeshuah is laid at the feet of one or another of the Judean factions, if not simply the Jews collectively. John Dominic Crossan's exhaustive research and analysis of the crucifixion narratives [3] makes it clear that the narratives, which he called "prophecy historicized," contributed mightily to anti-Semitism.

Besides, it would likely have been extremely risky for gospel compilers during the last third of the first century to accuse Rome of an unjust execution. Since the goal of their persecuted communities was hardly that of strengthening traditional Judaism, and since Yeshuah Judaism was in the business of trying to distinguish itself from synagogue Judaism, why not blame Yeshuah's death on the Jews?

From the next generation of the split-off movement emerged a fellow named Irenaeus. He was known as the Bishop of Lyons, and in the late second century he came out strong for what he called "orthodoxy" (from *ortho*, "right" or "straight," and *doxa*, "opinion" or "judgment"), a closely defined and monitored system of belief from which no divergence would be allowed. It was Irenaeus who championed the primacy of the Hellenistic John at the expense of the more humanist Mark, Matthew, Luke, and especially Thomas. John posits Yeshuah as the unseen and unseeable god in the flesh. Thomas depicts a very earthly and indeed earthy Jesus.[4]

While Irenaeus did not write for Jews, his heavy preference for the Jesus of John would not have escaped Jewish attention, and one can imagine their negative reaction. Irenaeus held that by refusing to accept Jesus in the terms found in John 1:1–14 ("the God who had spoken in human form"), the Jews had excluded themselves. Irenaeus went on to say that God disinherited the Jews and stripped them of their right to be his priests. They might continue to perform their priestly acts, but such acts would be invalid and worthless shams. In his time, Irenaeus was one of the most visible and audible spokespersons in what by then was known as "the church." His work is to this day deemed definitive by the church's most conservative theologians.

And 150 years after Irenaeus, Yeshuah Judaism—now known as "the church" or "Christianity"—had, to use the idiom of our time, been taken public. When, in 312–313 CE, Constantine found himself still standing as the last of a quartet of contenders for the imperial crown, he looked around at his vast empire and saw it hopelessly divided by language, culture, and religion. Competing brands of the "catholic" or "universal" church were at ideological loggerheads. Constantine was evidently a very astute fellow. He decided to take religious conflict, one of his greatest liabilities, and turn it into his greatest asset. So in 313, he issued the famous "Edict of Toleration," according to which the church was no longer to be persecuted, but rather tolerated.

Constantine still had a problem. The church was involved in an ecclesiastical civil war. Several branches and sects had not accepted the ironclad fundamentalism of Irenaeus and insisted that some biblical language—for example, portions of John—could and should be interpreted metaphorically. In short, they believed that the so-called "orthodox faith" was an acceptable beginning, but that a useful religion would have to be far more intellectually mature. There was also the dissenting party of post-Irenaeans led by Alexander of Alexandria and his faithful lieutenant, Athanasius. Apparently, Constantine did not care one way or the other how the theological conflicts got reconciled. He just wanted the church to settle on what had to be believed and enforced. So he summoned the regional overseers or superintendents of the church to a riparian city then called Nicaea, on the site of which now stands the village of Iznik at the eastern end of Sea of Maramara.

The imperial charge to the overseers was to come to an agreement on a creedal statement that would codify or set straight the church's teaching—literally, make it orthodox, as in orthodontics. At issue was whether Yeshuah, now called Christos, was of the same substance as god or of a similar substance. The post-Irenaean party led by Athanasius successfully championed the former, and so was promulgated in the infamous Nicene Creed. Therein,

Constantine, the recent convert, had his answer. All who did not believe that Yeshuah-was-Christos-was-God were to be condemned. Unrepentant Jews were among the first to feel the lash. By imperial edict, Jews were forbidden even to enter Jerusalem, save on the one day of their ritual mourning for a lost home. Jews who attempted to interfere with other Jews converting to Christianity were to be summarily executed.

It remained for Theodosius some eighty years later to drop the other shoe by giving the church full imperial status and by making it the one acceptable religious institution. Thus did Christian leaders of the time come to believe they had successfully effected a supersession—not only by invalidating Judaism by fiat, but also by demonizing its continuing adherents. It is little wonder that Christian orthodoxy would perpetuate anti-Semitism throughout the Middle Ages. It would be found in the formative work of Aquinas and notoriously in the work of Martin Luther.

Now recall those five thousand Jews or Judeans who were relocated from the Middle East to Italy by Titus post-70 CE. The archaeological record suggests that between the third and seventh centuries of the Common Era, those Jews lived in relative peace and concord with their non-Jewish neighbors. So assimilated were they that most inscriptions on burial slabs are in Greek, and of what Hebrew script has been found, most of the characters appear to spell out Greek and Latin transliterations. According to Colafemmina, the area around what is now Venosa was a prosperous center of trade, and its transplanted Jews played an important role in that business. Colafemmina says that by the end of the fourth century CE, many of the settlements were dominated by Jews who became political and community leaders. Yet Jews were expelled from what was then known as the Kingdom of Naples in the fifteenth century—at a time when orthodoxy and definition, including texts that could be interpreted as anti-Semitic, were being reasserted in the religious politics and prejudices of Europe. Such, then, is ample evidence of the gross misuse of texts that are attributed to divine origin, enforceable by a priestly elite, and as such beyond debate by human beings. Violence and death have been the direct effects of such misrepresentations. Unless and until proponents of the influential religions abandon claims of exclusive revelation and truth in their texts, the world will be unsafe. America's Founding Parents had a sense of that when they deliberately created a secular republic.

Notes

1. The visiting professor of Hebraic literature at the University of Calabria. See Brooks, "In Italian Dust, Signs of a Past Jewish Life."
2. For more on this subject, see Cook, *Seven Sayings of Jesus*.
3. Crossan, *Who Killed Jesus*.
4. Pagels, *Beyond Belief,* 29–75.

CHAPTER 8

Reclaiming Our Secular Humanist Origins

It is neither desirable nor possible in a secular democracy to attempt to force proponents of any religion to hide their lights under a bushel. In the kind of nation America ideally is, religion is 100 percent entrepreneurial. Anybody can found a religious community espousing a set of ideas of teachings and attempt to gain a following. The judicial system appears to go out of its way to afford as much latitude to religionists as public safety will permit. As things presently stand, one could not use the freedom of religion clause of the First Amendment to defend infant sacrifice as part of the weekly worship service. Nor are adherents of certain sects permitted to withhold treatment from minor children suffering from life-threatening maladies. Commonsense zoning ordinances govern land use and building codes for religious institutions as well as businesses and residences. But beyond that, religionists more or less have the sky as their limit. And not a straw should be laid in their path as they set out to convert the multitudes to their particular vision and to tutor their flocks in the teachings of their order. That is the genius of the First Amendment, and if apostles of the marketplace economy want a prime example of how it works, they need only look at the flourishing of religion in America. One can scarcely drive a city block without coming across one or more churches or other places of worship, each having its own bulletin board advertising whatever is offered within. The law should always and ever be construed as permitting and even encouraging such freedom.

For some religionists, though, that is not enough. It is not enough for them to have nearly unfettered freedom to celebrate their liturgies and preach their sermons and teach their catechisms to those who will endure them. They must have special rights and freedoms that go beyond the terms of the First Amendment. Among these complainants, some evangelical Christians insist that America was and is primarily a "Christian nation," founded broadly on biblical warrant. They pine for the era in which the public school day began with a recitation of the Lord's Prayer and a reading from the Jewish-Christian scriptures—practices that went unchallenged for a long while in a nation made up largely of white Protestant Americans. Those evangelicals rue the day the U.S. Supreme Court in a 1963 decision[1] ruled that sectarian prayer and Bible readings were unconsitutional in public schools that had long since acquired a religiously pluralistic population.

The evangelicals blame that decision for what they claim to see as a nearly fifty-year-long moral collapse. The unseemly spectacle that went on during the late summer of 2003 as a justice of the Alabama Supreme Court tried to defend the presence of a monument featuring the Ten Commandments in the rotunda of the state courthouse was part and parcel of such claims. The mob hysteria that narrow Christian fundamentalist leaders demagogued over the issue of the monument was a discouragement to civil libertarians everywhere.

The controversy over *Roe v. Wade*,[2] now in its fifth decade, is likewise a production of the Protestant and Roman

Catholic Right, whose exponents claim to see in the admittedly complicated ruling a legalization of murder, which is abhorrent not only to bible-believing and pope-obeying Christians, but to all civilized people. They also refuse to recognize the many and troublesome ambiguities inherent in the issue of abortion, two of which are the question of a woman's freedom to exercise control over her own body and the potential viability of a human embryo. The initiatives mounted by evangelicals and Catholics in response to their religious leaders to overturn *Roe v. Wade* on religious and theological grounds are a very real challenge to secular democracy. One must acknowledge that the religious arguments against slavery now embraced by civil libertarians involved a similar dilemma. Yet in both cases it is the freedom and dignity of a living individual—clearly a humanist principle—that is in question. The so-called Right-to-Life lobby, though, insists on the basis of church doctrine that the conceived embryo possesses those same rights in distinction from the woman in whose uterus the embryo is growing. It would be easier to engage in the debate if the Right-to-Lifers would apply Abraham Lincoln's take on slavery: "As I would not be a slave, so I would not be a master." Then the abortion debate could proceed on humanist grounds, and perhaps more people would join the discussion in the hope that it would partake in reason.

Nor will the Religious Right be satisfied until the courts or Congress makes it once again lawful for sectarian prayer to be offered in public school classrooms. All too frequently, one reads of some school district somewhere in which proponents of one religion or another are agitating or bringing suit to permit such pious exercises on the grounds of religious freedom. They countenance no argument to the effect that there are millions upon millions of hearths and homes and churches and masjids and temples in which prayer can be and certainly is offered many times daily. They scoff at the idea that in America any individual is free to pray to whatever deity or deities he or she envisions at any time and in any place as long as the praying does not impinge upon believers in other deities or upon nonbelievers or those who would be inconvenienced or endangered by the form of the prayer.

That, of course, is the point. It is not the freedom to pray that the complainants are really concerned about. They wish to make a public show of their praying (audiovisually, if possible) because they seem to believe that it is part of their required witness to the One God and His Will and Law and Ordinances, etc., etc. Their prayer, then, is to be a demonstration of their faith and their conviction that they are right and possess an exclusive revelation of what is so. And where better than in a clearly public venue? For using a space or building owned by the public through one of its branches of government will the more effectively punctuate the event with the message that this is, by God, a Christian nation! The same can be said of the nudging of the Religious Right yet again to include Bible readings in public schools. There again is the assertion of a religious chauvinism. The uncritical reading of Bible texts is one not-so-subtle way to reinforce the idea that those texts present nothing but inexorable truth.

Along the same lines is the push to include creationism or intelligent design in public school science curricula. The argument generally made is that evolution is just a theory. (They never use the term "natural selection," the concept that Charles Darwin reluctantly discerned from painstaking and unmistakable observation.) And, in their view, since evolution is just a theory, why not teach yet another theory? What's fair is fair. Of course, natural selection is not "just a theory," because the designation "theory" in the disciplines of science is not easily conferred upon an idea. A theory is a hypothesis that has been tested time and again in an attempt to disprove it. Such a hypothesis begins its life as a surmise based on some observation of data that led the investigator to posit an idea or principle as truth. Then the hypothesis is subjected unmercifully to test after test to see how it holds up. Only after all conceivable and available means to disprove it have been exhausted, only after it seems to explain cogently how such-and-such a thing is true, is it granted the exalted title "Theory" and a status rarely accorded by twenty-first century science—Evolution, Special, and General Relativity being three of the few. It is, of course, impossible to subject "creationism" or its allegedly more sophisticated cousin "intelligent design" to the rigors of the laboratory because they are essentially deductive in nature. They begin by presupposing a theistic belief and then marshal the data to prove that life is the product of divine wisdom and order.

I grew up in a world in which the biblical doctrine of creation was taken for granted, and I admit that, at ten years of age, I was enormously comfortable with it. Public school education eventually helped me see that what I was taught in Sunday school did not represent what was so. I found, though, that the fault was in me. I must admit that none of my Sunday school teachers tried to convince me or my peers that Genesis represented a scientific explanation of how the world came into existence. It was my own surmise that a document called "the Word of God" would not mince words about truth. And, therein, of course, is the difficulty with religious texts and their inappropriate use. Combined with religious activities such as prayer, they belong in the religious venue, where priests and ministers and rabbis and imams may preach what they please and teach what they will to people who will hear what they hear and respond as they respond. But in public venues, such documents as the Bible must be treated as historical, literary artifacts[3] that may or may not convey truth. In any case, whatever supposed truth they are perceived to convey must be subjected to the same objective rigors as any other assertions of truth.

Another wrinkle in this time of cultivated confusion among religious and public matters is the widely debated issue of "faith-based operations," a major rallying point in the 2000 campaign of George W. Bush and, in a somewhat diminished way, an early feature of his administration. In a naked attempt to foster the interests of religion, the Bush camp advocated government financial support of social services performed by religious institutions. Such an advocacy is an unmistakable feature of the privatization efforts of the conservative movement. (May the Fates forfend that government should be involved in the delivery of any services but national defense!) Not only should churches and other religious groups do what their social commitments would lead them to do—thus relieving government of the need to respond to human need—but how better for government to reward the religious communities of the nation with financial support, given that Christian communities would constitute the vast majority of those that might qualify. America is, after all, "a Christian nation."

To reclaim the secular and humanist nature of the American nation—which reclamation may well be the key to its survival as a democracy—the people will have to rebuff the blandishments of conservative politicians who seek to inject into government and governance an essentially evangelical tone and purpose. They will have to recognize that the public square is the absolutely appropriate site for the edifices of religious institutions, but they will have to insist that such institutions observe the principles of market economy: Advertise, sell, attempt to convince and persuade—but do it on your own and with your own resources. Make such a case for your ideology that people will throng to its outward and visible signs. And may the most effective religion get the glory. In the town in which I live, the best-attended non-Roman Catholic congregation is the Salvation Army citadel. Why? Because people believe it is always doing something to make the gospel real in the lives of the poor and disadvantaged. That's what they tell me, anyway, and that's the American way.

The United States of America is a secular democracy grounded in the insights of the Greek philosophers who celebrated human potential and initiative. Where seventeenth- and eighteenth-century Christianity lifted up and affirmed the values inherent in those philosophies, Christianity was affirmed. The "certain inalienable rights" referenced in the Declaration of Independence, and the humanist values expressed in Lincoln's Gettysburg and Second Inaugural Addresses are echoed in Jewish and Christian, Muslim, and Buddhist scriptures. But they are fundamentally human values, not overtly sectarian or religious pronouncements.

It may seem ironic to some that religion, especially in its institutional forms, has flourished in America more than in any other modern nation because—and especially because—the nation's founding and maturing has valued freedom of and from religion. The key reason for this phenomenon is the free marketplace of ideas. We can reclaim our secular origins by insisting on the marketplace economy for religion in all its overt forms. Religion must—and religions must—compete for human allegiance. Religious texts must be kept and taught within the communities that value and cherish them—or if they are to enter the public sphere, be subject to literary and historical criticism, as any other texts would be. No single religion or religious expression must ever be favored overtly or covertly by any level of government, or the whole noble experiment will be ruined. The place of religion in a secular society must be an entirely private matter, for people must be free to decide whether or not to attend or affiliate themselves with one or more of its several institutions that are perceived from time to time to meet certain human needs in a way that makes them attractive.

See the typical village square around which, in countless American communities, one may find several buildings with distinctive denominational loyalties, peopled on prescribed holy days for prescribed rituals and teaching. See also on that square the town hall and the library. These latter two are owned by all. The houses of worship belong to those who belong to them. All citizens of the village are welcomed in the town hall and the library, because both belong to all. What is preached and taught in Church A is for the members and inquirers of Church A. If one doesn't like the message, there is always Church B—or the library for those who are independent inquirers. Such a model of civil maturity and peace could, if left alone, become the envy of a world that is presently choked with the kind of deadly religious sentiments that lead at least to exclusion, and at worst to violence and death.

Notes

1. *Abington Township School District v. Schempp* 374 U.S. 203 1963.
2. 410 U.S. 113 1973.
3. In his majority opinion in *Abington v. Schemmp* (joined with *Murray v. Curlett*), Justice Tom Clark wrote: "It certainly may be said that the Bible is worthy of study for its literary and historic quali-

ties. Nothing we have said here indicates that such study of the Bible or of religion, when presented objectively as part of as secular program of education, may not be effected consistent with the First Amendment."

CHAPTER

9

Religion as a Search for Meaning

If religion is anything useful, it is a search for meaning in life. Generations of human beings in varied cultural settings around the world have sought meaning in the repetition of rituals that involve the chanting of supposedly sacred texts and priestly interpretation of the same to the laity. Practitioners of both Eastern and Western varieties of religion have established rites of prayer and meditation in the performance of which they say they are trying to commune or communicate with and respond to powerful, unseen entities that are said to exist. Some people find meaning for themselves in such activities, and that is as it should be. But problems arise when they take up the task of finding meaning for someone else in their religious activities.

In whatever form it takes, whether in Hinduism, Judaism, Christianity, or Islam, the evangelical fervor of the true believer is an awesome thing to behold. How much better it would be if the purveyors of a religion would practice it in the "let-your-light-so-shine-before-men-that-they-may-see-your-good-works" way, and let the flies come to the honey rather than hunting them down one by one and compelling them to ingest it. The assumption that religion in general is good for everybody, or that one among the

85

many of them is better than the rest, is dangerous. It too easily results in the kind of disastrous ideology-turned-policy that guided (or misguided) the United States in the 1960s and '70s in its attempt to institute Western-style democracy in Vietnam. The ultimate downside of that notion was nowhere more exquisitely expressed than in the infamous military assessment: "We had to destroy the village in order to save it."

The Midwestern hamlet in which I grew up consisted of slightly fewer than one thousand people and boasted three and a half churches. The half stands for the Episcopal Church, which sometimes existed as an institution and sometimes did not—there being no permanent edifice or assigned clergyman. The other choices were the Roman Catholic mission, the Methodist Church, and a weekly gathering known as the Pilgrim Holiness Church. People were frowned upon who did not have at least nominal membership in one of these groups. And it was also a good idea to show up on more than just Christmas and Easter. By the time the Cold War had spawned the hysteria of the McCarthyist campaign against "godless communism," you were suspect if you did not sport some clear (and acceptable) religious affiliation.

I give credit to the clergy leaders of those churches during those years. They did not proselytize—not even the Pilgrim Holiness minister who was otherwise known for his fiery sermons. He seemed content to damn to perdition the less-than-faithful among his own flock and to leave the rest of us alone. It was the palpable pressure exerted by the community as a whole that made it incumbent upon the merchant who would vend his wares to the village populace to show up in church with some regularity. My late father was an attorney in the village, and I am not sure to this day how much general approbation he thought he required in order to earn a decent living or to what extent he cared about what people thought of him. He did go to church, though he was unsparing of the pastor and the pastor's execrable sermons—and I clearly recall that "execrable" was the adjective my father used to describe those homiletic forays. I think it is safe to say that father derived little meaning for his life out of showing up in the pew, stumbling along with the pious nineteenth-century hymnody, repeating the prayers, and enduring the pastor's pointless harangues. But he insisted that we should go because "it builds character."

At sixteen years of age, I was fortunate enough to encounter the rare public school teacher of that era—a retired farmer with University of Michigan undergraduate and graduate degrees. His name was John C. Young, and he introduced me to Shakespeare and Milton and to a world of literature about which theretofore I had known little. At about that same time, my first real girlfriend— an accomplished pianist by the time she was seven years old—went off for two weeks to Interlochen, which is now an internationally known academy of the arts. I accompanied her parents to her final recital and the year-end concert that the Youth Symphony presented, which included two movements of the Schubert Trout Quintet played by the top students in the string section.

There I discovered "meaning," the kind of "poetry" or "powerful feeling" whose source Samuel Coleridge had described as emotion recollected in tranquility. The combination of being tutored in the classics by Mr. Young and having Schubert, Mozart, Beethoven, Brahms, and Bach enter my life had put me in touch with what poet William Wordsworth called "a sense sublime / Of something far more deeply interfused...."[1] Later in my college and graduate school days and then on into my useful adulthood, I have found meaning in many forms of art, some of which I do not know as well as music and literature. "Meaning" here stands for the sense that the individual is part and parcel of a world in which indefinable sublimity coexists with savagery—the former being a way of coping with and even overcoming the latter.

One evening many years ago, a family of what we locals called "summer people" decided to inaugurate a regular Sunday night combination salon-musicale on their front lawn overlooking the lower end of the magnificent Torch Lake. There on an August evening, with a red sun still an hour from the western horizon setting afire a tier of cumulus clouds and gentle waves lapping upon the beach below, I saw and heard a pick-up string ensemble play one of Mozart's "Haydn Quartets." Later on, someone read a long section of the Wordsworth poem.

I had been that morning to church, of course, and heard a choir of spinsters hack out a version of "Bringing in the Sheaves" and the pastor tell us that if we didn't believe Jesus died to save our sins, hell was to be our final destination. Can you guess where I found meaning that counted for something that day? A couple of weeks later, I was back in school and sought out J. C. Young. I asked him why he thought the Mozart and the Wordsworth filled my young soul with joy and aspiration, and why church left me cold. He said, "Well, Mozart and Wordsworth only ask that you hear them. They don't tell you they are the only music or the only poetry. They don't compel you to be anything or do anything." I responded that, in fact, Mozart and Wordsworth did compel me to be good and gentle and aware of nature and of other people. Young, with a knowing smile, replied, "Then, listen to Mozart. Learn to play his music. Recite Wordsworth, and be whatever it makes you and go wherever it leads you."

Although I was enamored of Young's philosophy, years of training kept me seeking in church rituals for the meaning that otherwise came so easily with Mozart and Wordsworth—even though the music was seldom as good as I found on LP records, and the sermons continued to be as irrelevant as they were terrible. Then came my undergraduate days at a liberal arts college where I was fortunate to be just good enough to get a place in the bass section of the choral society. That ensemble had enough talent to sing Bach motets, Handel oratorios, and the like. Because of the college setting, the music in the local churches was better than I had ever heard, as were the sermons, which in topic and substance were more like the lectures I was hearing in the classroom and far less like the harangues I was accustomed to. That made me think that my earlier experiences with religion had simply been low-grade, and now I had found the real thing. A ministerial position came in my last year of graduate school when, for a field work assignment, I managed to get myself appointed assistant chaplain at a major university. There, too, the music and the sermons were excellent. Then, upon completion of my graduate degrees, I had to get a real job.

At only twenty-five years of age, I had ministry in what was a pretty insignificant appointment: a small-town Protestant church where the music would have been better imagined than performed and the congregation found my sermons a source of great consternation because they consisted more in the posing of inquiries and propositions than in pronouncements. All my efforts to form book clubs and study groups were met with kind bemusement. "Son," one of my parishioners said, "you're in the wrong business if you think that we come to church to learn stuff. You're wasting your time." And, of course, the choir and the organist were not only resistant to the simplest selections from the classical repertoire, but even if they had been willing, the results would have been anything but edifying. So maybe I was in the wrong business. That became much more apparent in my second and final years in that congregation. Having failed to get people to read and discuss the provocative books then being written,[2] I began to review them in sermons. Because each of those authors had made sound cases that theism might no longer be workable or even useful as a philosophy of religion—and because I made plain the implications of those well-made cases—the reactions of the congregation made it clear that I was on very thin ice.

My transfer to a large city congregation in 1967 and a subsequent ten-year stint found me in an inner-city parish just when the nation was coming to grips with the civil rights and antiwar movements, the urban riots of 1966 and 1967, the bitter controversy over Vietnam culminating in the Kent State massacre in 1970, and the national disillusionment over Watergate. These explosive issues diverted attention and energies from theological matters to the church's engagement in social and political action. Scholarship—and especially the publishing of its fruits—was often in temporary suspension as we turned our hands to the obvious tasks before us that resulted from ruined cities and dispirited peoples. It would be a while until such challenging figures as Marcus Borg, Elaine Pagels, John Dominic Crossan, and Paula Fredriksen began to issue the provocative works that called some of us from the field of social witness back to the more philosophical and intellectual inquiries that had held our attention in the years before. By then, of course, the forces of reaction had come to the fore in the various evangelical and fundamentalist communities, and questioning traditional religious thought and forms was no longer received as a curiosity, but rather as a sin against the Holy Ghost. The upsurge of the Christian Right was soon enough followed by the volcanic eruptions of fundamentalist Islam and Orthodox Judaism. In India, Hindus and Muslims went at each other hammer and tong. Religion was becoming the agent of death—again.

After an eight-and-a-half year interim as a reporter, editor, and columnist at a major newspaper, I returned in 1987 to parish ministry. I began slowly to take up the kind of initiative I had begun nearly a quarter of a century earlier. I introduced a suburban congregation to the idea that, as the Gershwin lyric goes, "It ain't necessarily so... The things that you're liable to read in the Bible, they ain't necessarily so." The going was rough for quite a while. I made it increasingly clear that inasmuch as I was not a theist, I was an a-theist. I early on dismissed as irrelevant the church's doctrines concerning Jesus' virgin birth, physical resurrection, and ascension. I questioned the efficacy of prayer beyond the opportunities it afforded for focus. I made plain the impossibility of treating the Bible as if it were somehow more (or less) than literature. I let my congregation in on my research that had led me to consider that, whoever the actual Jesus of Nazareth may have been, he had been hijacked by religious hucksters to mean anything they needed for him to mean. I published a book exposing all that for what it was and found the pews of my church missing a number of people. Two years later, I issued an anthology of homilies called *Sermons of a Devoted Heretic* and, two years after that, a book entitled *Seven Sayings of Jesus*, in which I made a case that rather than some kind of miracle worker, Jesus had been a teacher of ethical wisdom, and that all efforts to make him into some divine figure were ridiculous and maybe even dangerous. Curiously enough, in the latter years of my active ministry, the congregation I served had pretty much recovered from the earlier crisis provoked by my intellectual honesty, and partly because of it had in fact begun to prosper. More curious still was the decision from above not to try me for heresy. In almost any other era or epoch, I would have been convicted and subsequently defrocked; indeed, through the years many of my colleagues among the clergy would go out of their way to tell me what a kook I am, how mistaken my work is, and—the ultimate put-down—that "I just don't get it." I am told that my work is hopelessly representative of "modernism," and that the church is already into the "post-Modernist age"—whatever any of that may mean.

My answer to that is fairly radical. I reply that the church *qua* church is really on its last legs. The emptiness of much of its rites and rituals is more and more the clothing of a nonexistent emperor. Its pronouncements about what is true and right ring hollow, except to its diehard followers. The world will eventually come into its own and throw off the sacral thrall cast over it by the church and other religious movements and institutions, but its human inhabitants will have achieved what humanity is theirs through the search for and attainment of meaning. For too long, meaning has been sought, ultimately in vain, through the practice of religions that have posited the existence of an unseen god or gods whose will and law need to be mediated through a priestly elite. The abuses of such a system constitute much of the history of religion. By what means, then, are human beings to seek meaning for their lives?

A stable, fundamentally intelligent person cannot regard the plentitude of life and its bafflingly ordered nature without wondering about the cause or source of that order. One cannot see the images relayed by the Hubble Space Telescope and not wonder what the source of those trillions

-of-miles-high gas eruptions might be. We see order in the universe in events ranging from the startlingly predictable phenomena of sidereal time to the gestation of a human being. And we see what we take to be chaos, sometimes in monumental proportions, and yet it seems impossible to shrug our shoulders and chalk even that up to the random bouncing of molecules off one another. An inductive pursuit and examination of nature's data leads most people to posit some kind of source-ordering principle in the universe. The poet-philosopher who some 2,500 years ago gave us the famed "P" (Priestly) Document,[3] portions of which are scattered among the books of the Pentateuch, envisioned the source of the universe's substance as emerging from a primordial chaos, out of which an ordering principle wrought some measure of order. Modern science has been able to grasp that the substance and its ordering principle seem not to be as arbitrarily separable as we once imagined. Charles Darwin, among others, helped human beings appreciate the fact that, individually and corporately, they are part of both the substance and the evolving order—and ordering. A first-century Jew known as Saul of Tarsus intimated that human beings shared in the divine work.[4] We might say in a twenty-first century restatement of that sentiment that human beings seem, at their best, to participate with the universe in the ordering of life. While other cultures in other times and places have certainly produced order, the European Renaissance of the sixteenth and seventeenth centuries stands out as an example of how human beings can do more than simply react to life. They can master and manage it through the art and technology they have created.

Government with the consent of the governed—"of the people, by the people, and for the people"—may be the best opportunity thus far in the human experience to extend and maintain the kind of dependable order that creates an environment sufficiently secure to provide for advancement of the arts and sciences—and thus to enhance and fulfill the lives of all involved. It is within such an enterprise that one acceptable and adequate substitute for the word "god" can be found. "God" is simply an imperfect and misleading word standing for what is best in humanity, what is worth pursuing. The temples of such a "god" are the concert hall, the theater, the art gallery, the library, the lecture hall, the laboratory, and the corridors of enlightened government. The music that is made in them, the information and insight imparted in them, the beauty displayed in them, the experiments carried on in them, the laws defining and establishing standards of human behavior written in them—these all constitute the liturgy—or public work—of twenty-first century human beings who ennoble their lives as they share in the ordering of whatever elements of the universe's substance they have to hand.

Thus are we talking not theism, but humanism. Humanism invites the human being to consider that he or she partakes in the collective human potential. At the same time, humanists must face up to and acknowledge the individual and collective failures of their own kind. Conventional theistic religions direct their adherents to undertake complex liturgies of contrition for such inhumanity. But as we have said, humanism's liturgy is the purposive, egalitarian cultivation of the arts, of law, and of the sciences—pursuits that at their best produce works that seem to be greater than the sum of their parts. Such greatness can satisfy the human need for meaning as well as offering a rational foundation for the ethically sound behavior that theistic religions ineffectively attempt to provide.

If one wishes to say that humanism is a religion, let it be said. But it is a religion that does not direct its appeals to an unseen god or gods and is not mediated through a priestly elite. "Membership" is open to anyone who can and will participate and contribute, if only by staying in the conversation and learning, by advancing knowledge, and cultivating the arts. A five-year-old youngster learning to play the C-major scale on the piano is cultivating the arts. The parent who reads *Alice in Wonderland* to his or her children is advancing the cause of literacy and literary appreciation. The adult who pays attention to the affairs of government and who never misses a chance to cast an informed vote is contributing to the conservation of participatory democracy and thus makes possible the peaceful pursuit of meaning. Traditional religions and religious institutions will continue to exist and from time to time prosper. But they must exist in and for themselves and not be allowed to infringe upon the freedom of those who reject their theologies and resist their supernatural interpretation of data. In a secular society, any idea, concept, or proposition is like the scientist's hypothesis: It is offered in order to be tested, and is subject to being proven wrong, invalid, or unworkable. American Christians who rejoice in a supposed numerical hegemony in fact possess something far better: a set of ethical hypotheses that they would do well to offer to the world. These are expressed in a series of sayings that most New Testament scholars are willing to attribute to the figure known as Jesus of Nazareth. They are:

Turn the other cheek.

Walk the second mile.

Give up your shirt as well as your coat.

Forgive seventy times seven times (i.e., as often it takes).

Love your neighbor.

Love your enemy.

Treat others as you want them to treat you.

The hypothesis is that if one practices the principles embodied in these sayings, he or she will set forth a countercultural ethos that will, over time, attract others to that ethos because the ethos seems to work. Stable and sane human beings like nothing better than something that works, that produces desirable results and nurtures security. This ethos relies on no references to unseen powers; it requires no priesthood to mediate it; it needs only lived-out practice in the everyday affairs of people so that it increasingly becomes the norm. The fact is that each of the principles set forth in those brief sayings can be found here and there in religious literature and tradition other than the Judeo-Christian. That means, of course, that the principles are in some way fundamental to the better nature of human beings everywhere. While both Judaism and Christianity locate the origins of the ethos in divine initiative, the above-noted evidence suggests that it is more likely to have evolved among people trying to survive by getting along and seeking common goals.

One need look no further than Genesis 4 for a major clue that even the thinkers who gave us early portions of that collection of documents located the origins of its ethos in human history. In as pointed a myth as was ever devised, Cain, the first brother, has killed his sibling, Abel, because Cain believes that god has been pleased with Abel's sacrifice but displeased with his own. That deed attracts the attention of the god Yahweh, who asks, "Where is your brother?" Then, after the first lie has been told and summarily disallowed, comes the dreaded accusatory question repeated in anguish billions of times by horrified parents and other authority figures: "What have you done?" The question was not "What have you believed?" or "What is your theology?" but "What have you done?" How have you behaved, and why? That is what counts in the real world.

From the early days of this tradition, then, comes a clue that has been tragically overlooked by too many for too long. Too much time and energy have been expended on figuring out what to believe, what rituals to perform, and in what manner—and not nearly enough on how to treat one another. A humanist religion in a secular society may well have a more important place than ever before if it mines its textual traditions for the behavioral wisdom that will be necessary if human beings are not to destroy their civilization piece by piece, and along with it this fragile planet they call home.

Notes

1. Wordsworth, "Lines Composed A Few Miles Above Tintern Abbey," ll. 95–96.

2. Among them, *The Secular City* by Harvey Cox, *The Secular Meaning of the Gospel* by Paul M. van Buren, *The Gospel of Christian Atheism* by Thomas Altizer, and *Honest To God* by John A.T. Robinson—to name but four of the dozen or so volumes that were then reshaping religious thought in the English-speaking world.

3. The so-called "documentary hypothesis" developed by Julius Wellhausen (1844–1918) and with which virtually all biblical scholars concur, holds that the Pentateuch is a compilation of four or more independent, sometimes parallel narratives combined into its current form by a series of redactors. The number of these is usually set at four, but this is not an essential part of the hypothesis. The primary resources the hypothesis posits are the Jahwist (J), so called for its use of the Hebrew *Jahweh* for "God," dating to as early as the tenth century BCE; along with the Elohist (E), so called for the use of *Elohim* for "Gods"; the Deuteronomist (D); and the Priestly source (P), dating to the eighth to sixth centuries. The final compilation of the extant text is generally dated to either the sixth or fifth century BCE.

4. 1 Corinthians 3:9, 2 Corinthians 6:1.

CHAPTER

10

A Nontheistic Ethic of Restraint and a Commitment to Inquiry

When stirrings of what would become the Enlightenment first began to be felt, Francis Bacon and Galileo Galilei were prominent among those who began to impose upon claims of truth the discipline of testing by observation and experiment. With that, the end was in sight for theistic religion and its authoritarian claims appealing to unseen gods and revealed truth. Religion that is be taken seriously in the twenty-first century will have to back away from its exaggerated claims for supposedly sacred texts that in fact are beyond warrant and commonsense; give up the certitude of "god-talk"; and seek common cause with other branches of human inquiry by embracing the natural ambiguity and relativism that comes with human finitude and inability to comprehend the whole of things. In short, it must accustom itself to honoring and encouraging doubt, skepticism, and questioning as desirable human qualities.

Anthropological and archaeological records demonstrate that the phenomenon of religion in the human epoch can be traced to disparate sources (see Chapter V). One such factor is the worship of ancestors by succeeding generations who, in seeking to control their societies, appealed to the received wisdom vouchsafed to them by dead elders. Perhaps to answer doubt among younger members of the tribe or clan that such elders knew what they were talking about, adult members erected shrines to the memories of predecessors by then unseen. It does not take much imagination to see how that process evolved into a full-blown worship of "gods." The mystique of sacramental rites administered and withheld provided a means of control over people in creating and maintaining some semblance of societal order.

As agricultural communities replaced hunter-gatherer societies, social organization began to take the shape of loosely related tribes. As any community does, those groups required both authority structures and a division of labor, no doubt involving a greater degree of control than had previously been needed. It makes sense to suppose that, at this point, priesthoods emerged as guardians of the memories and enforcers of the order derived from them. In a good many ancient societies, priests seem to have been partly in thrall to military and political leaders—an association that would become all too common in later times. In a scenario posited earlier—the elders of a primitive community sitting around the central fire pit mulling over how to organize their common life—it is possible to imagine one of them observing that the natural urge to want something that belongs to another can lead to theft and ultimately to violence and even death. Therefore, it might well have been decreed, covetousness is to be discouraged and perhaps replaced by a work ethic that could enable a would-be coveter to earn for himself what he might otherwise have coveted. That would reduce the incidence of theft, violence, and murder. One can see some of the "thou shalt nots" forming up, and along with them what many, many centuries later would be denominated *religare,* or intentional restraint: that is, religion with a clearly ethical content.

However, restraint is what much of contemporary religious expressions lack as their leaders compete with one another to claim possession of exclusive truth. We are told that angry young Muslim men are content to blow themselves up in terrorist attacks because it is the will of Allah that the infidel societies of the West should be destroyed. The preachers on American cable television are just as certain that the god of the Christian Bible is proclaiming through them a set of inexorable truths that must be accepted by one and all to ensure their eternal salvation and to spare them eternal damnation. This is not restraint. Restraint is finding within one's own religious belief system those elements and strategies that have been successful and putting them into practice as examples others might wish to follow because their desirability has been demonstrated. One readily thinks, for example, of Hillel the Elder's advice: "What you hate, do not do to another."

As written language took hold in the societies of antiquity, the setting down of laws and covenants, stories, and liturgical texts was bound to occur. The provenance of each could no doubt have been traced to the "memories" of early communities—reported recollections of the wisdom of unseen (that is to say, dead) ancestors. But much as dead ancestors morphed into "gods," so the written record of the law that evolved in these emergent communities became sacred writ. It fell, of course, to the priests to mediate those texts and thereby to consolidate their power and authority. The text meant what the priests said it meant because their exalted station bestowed on them a kind of *gnosis* not accessible to the masses. One can draw an almost direct line from the priests of antiquity to the fundamentalist preachers of our own era, who, despite their denial of the validity of the office, amount to a Protestant papacy whose members tell their congregations that the Bible means what it says and says what it means.

Fundamentalist interpretations of so-called sacred texts enabled the bloody Crusades, abetted the church's demonization of Galileo, fueled the Inquisition and its latter-day extension under the contemporary papacy, and inspired the legislatures of several U.S. states to attempt to make illegal the teaching of evolutionary biology in public schools. Incredible as it may seem, the scientific knowledge that empowers the modern practice of medicine is being called into question solely on the grounds that the long-accepted Theory of Natural Selection and the science that has flowed from its exhaustive testing do not conform to sacred texts.

The assertion that any or all of the biblical documents have any origin other than the human imagination is beyond ludicrous. Yet that claim is made in a fashion credible to millions of people every day by exponents of one fundamentalism or another. What, then, shall religious exponents say of their cherished texts if they cannot claim them to have been revealed and therefore beyond challenge? They can say that such texts are repositories of human experience, inquiry, investigation, acquired wisdom; that many of passages in them are possessed of great lyrical beauty and astonishing insight worth paying attention to and considering in the making of important choices and decisions.

Imagine the relaxation of tension and conflict in the world if only religious leaders of the various communities of faith were to refrain from claiming absolute and exclusive truth for their sacred texts. The energy now spent in the aggressive defense of the content of such texts could be channeled into packaging it for display and vending in the marketplace of ideas. To those who might complain that such a strategy would be an open door to syncretism, I say simply that sectarianism certainly hasn't worked very well. Let's try a new way. Peace is preferable to war, calm to conflict, intelligent discussion to fevered controversy, light to heat.

Advocacy of a next logical step might consist in inviting readers to recall a philosophical development that was *au courant* forty years ago, one that arose from the research and writing of such scholars as Paul M. van Buren, Gabriel Vahanian, Harvey Cox, and Thomas Altizer. The popular press dubbed it the "Death of God" movement, but it was not a movement, and it did nothing close to writing any god's obituary. The argument was that "god talk" had become ever more difficult in the wake of the Enlightenment, since the work of Copernicus, Galileo, Newton, Darwin, and Einstein had pretty much dismantled the universe of antiquity. A further argument was that the Holocaust and other dread episodes of human misbehavior—man's inhumanity to man—had rendered the conventional concepts of god incredible. Adopting the fashion of David Hume, van Buren in particular argued that human beings might more sensibly focus their attention on what could be apprehended by the senses and subsequently submitted to reason—namely, one another and the general affairs of humankind—and seek therein cues to further consideration and consequent action.

The perils inherent in god-talk were not as obvious forty years ago as they are now. As fundamentalists across the religious spectrum have turned up the decibel level of their claims to truth, Allah, Yahweh, and whatever god it is that Roman Catholic and Protestant Christians posit seem to be in lively competition with one another. The late Osama bin Laden invoked and his followers continue to invoke Allah in merciless acts of terrorism. American evangelicals advocate a weird alchemy of theism and patriotism in support of the war of attrition in Afghanistan and various other ideological endeavors. The Christian Right invokes the god of the Bible in its battle to fill up the seats of the U.S. Supreme Court with justices deemed to be supportive of conservative causes.

The trouble with god-talk of any sort is that it renders moot any attempt at debate. When, for example, a television preacher tells you that the god he worships—and believes to be the only and almighty god—wills the passage of a constitutional amendment to outlaw abortion, he is appealing to an unseen source of authority above and beyond the abilities of investigation, research, and reason. When the Muslim fanatic speaks the name of Allah just prior to pulling the pin on his vest bomb, argument is terminated. Allah speaks, the terrorist believes; *ergo*, the resultant blast. Hindus and Muslims cheerfully cut each other to ribbons, over which what's left of them will occupy some site considered holy by both of them, but blessed by opposing gods. This is no way to run a world.

Like his contemporaries of the mid-1960s, van Buren advocated a moratorium on god-talk until such time as those who would speak thus could get their semantic and philosophical houses in sufficient order as to be able to use language that would not be ludicrous in the face of commonly accepted reality. Paul Tillich, who died in 1965 at about the time that van Buren and the others were publishing, had offered his own guarded version of god-talk. Tillich wrote persuasively of what he called "the Ground and Source of Being" and was fond of answering the sophomoric question, "Does God exist?" with a stern "Nein!" When he used the word "god," Tillich generally connected it to his phrase "the uncreated creator." Following Tillich's lead, I crafted the term "source-orderer" and, in *Christianity Beyond Creeds,* used it to account for the fact that there is something rather than nothing, and that much of what is gives evidence of sometimes exquisite order. Farther than that, I was and am unwilling to go.

The trouble with going any farther is that all too soon anthropocentric characteristics are attributed to a source-orderer, and the discourse becomes reflective of whoever is doing the attributing. Naturally enough, a white, male, middle-class attributor will cast "god" in his own image. Furthermore, the attributor will miraculously discover that his "god" likes things the way he himself likes them. It is obvious what happens when the "god" of one cultural experience bumps up against a "god" of an opposing cultural experience. It is ridiculous on the face of it to have human beings in the twenty-first century debating—or worse yet taking up arms—over what "god" wills or which of the several posited "gods" is the real one.

Thus van Buren and company were not wrong to have proposed a moratorium on god-talk. Their work, in fact, was brilliant. So why, after the fifteen-minutes-of-fame treatment the media gave it, did it fade from public attention? My hypothesis, based on the axiom that timing is everything, is that their ground-breaking philosophical work was pushed into the background by the simultaneous explosions of the civil rights and antiwar movements, along with the sexual revolution—three eruptions that had all of America by the ears for most of the ensuing decade. By the time things settled down after Watergate, evangelical fundamentalism and the conservative movement in politics were in the ascendant, and no tolerance could be allowed for the embrace of ambiguity and continued inquiry. By then, everything was in the "answer mode."

The exponential growth of the mega-church movement in America, the even greater expansion of what Penn State scholar Philip Jenkins calls "southern Christianity"[1] in Africa, Asia, and Pacific Rim nations, the potentially explosive tensions of post-Reagan/Thatcher/Bush political analysis—these unsettling developments have left little room for the kind of no-holds-barred probing and bold questioning that the religious philosophers of the mid-1960s undertook. The perils of failing to probe and question are obvious, and this book is a call to the religious community to resume that kind of work and to compete in the public square for attention to its fruitful outcomes. A religion that refuses to undertake critical examination of its beliefs and practices is far more a problem than a solution.

For what rational and useful purpose can a religious movement, organization, or community exist? What would "pay its rent," justify its existence? Since the real property and buildings of not-for-profit religious institutions are exempt from taxation by local, state, or federal governments, should not such institutions arrange their work to benefit the communities in which they are established? Inasmuch as the First Amendment to the U.S. Constitution and the whole body of law that has developed under it leave religious groups free to teach and preach to their willing congregants what they please (this side of sedition), they could as well be centers for critical thinking. Synagogues, churches, mosques, and temples do not exist in a vacuum. Their members live and move and have their being in neighborhoods and communities. Every major religion conserves a history and a literature that could serve as a basis for critical thinking, setting aside theological and ritual convention long enough to help people use the lenses of those historical texts to focus on how they might live in peace and security with one another.

Communities centered on a religious tradition are ideal venues for encouraging a local, regional, national, and multinational politics of integrity. Surely they could contribute to the rebuilding and repopulating of decayed American cities; the encouragement of academic freedom, scientific investigation and research; the fostering of a societal commitment to peace and economic justice; and the nurturing of the arts, the humanities, and an aggressively free press. And these, together with the carefully nurtured guarantee of civil liberties, comprise the very soul of a democracy.

Such religious communities, having foresworn claims to the possession of revealed truth, meaningless and divisive god-talk, and sectarianism in all its forms, would glow like a welcome lamp in an otherwise depressing darkness. They would be temples rededicated to the amazing power and potential of reason in the midst of the chaos of unreason that hold in its deadly grip much of institutional and "movement" religion. The life of such communities would be a celebration of the human capacity to use doubt creatively, of the freedom to question and analyze.

Note

1. Jenkins, *The Next Christendom*.

CHAPTER

11

The Humanist's Goal Is Becoming Human

It is assumed that each of us is born human. Those who are zealous to curtail women's reproductive rights insist that from the time of conception, the embryo is fully human with all the civil rights of a person. Be that as it may, the reality of the matter is that an embryo or a fetus or an infant is always in the process of becoming human, and that is why good parenting is considered to be vital to society as a whole as well as to individual offspring. It is pretty much the consensus of the child psychology community that genes, while determinative in some ways, share the dynamics of child development with environment and the effect of education and socialization. John Donne had a hold on a piece of the truth about human beings when he wrote, "No man is an island, entire of itself; every man is a piece of the continent, a part of the main... [for all are] involved in mankind."[1]

William Golding's *Lord of the Flies* went so far as to suggest that, without the constraints and salutary influences of responsible communities, civilization can quickly devolve into savagery. Thus it is that the individual human being is ever in the process of formation, being influenced by what he or she sees, hears, touches, tastes, and smells. Over time, the individual becomes a full-fledged adult, but even at majority never escapes the stimuli of life around him. He or she will become one kind of person or another, depending in considerable measure on what those stimuli are.

A child born into a family where books abound and where parents and older siblings read and discuss what they are reading, a family whose members care for and support one another and respect familial, neighborhood, civic, and political responsibilities, that child stands a better than even chance of emerging into a useful adulthood. And if exposed to the finer arts as a child, if encouraged and supported in practicing an instrument, taking voice lessons, or learning to paint, he or she will enter adulthood as a fuller person than one who grows up under less advantageous circumstances.

If one is born into a family whose adults take seriously the values of community solidarity, peace, and justice and who communicate by precept and example the principles and lineaments of those values to their children, then those children—barring some mental or psychological disorder—will embody such values. They will, in fact, become human. They were not born human in more than a biological sense, and unless reared in a responsible way, they will never be human in any but a generic sense.

The process of becoming human is one of works, not faith. It is a courage-based initiative with the following principles uppermost:

1. Reliance on reason in commonsense decision making and conduct; acting on the basis of learned and considered experience both personal and communal.
2. Respect for the dignity of self and other human beings regardless of who they are racially, culturally, sexually, politically, or economically.

3. Acknowledgement that the biosphere is not of human making, that human beings have evolved within the evolution of its biological life, and that they share its resources with other life forms.
4. Stewardship of the environment—the atmosphere, the water, and the land—that as the common home to human beings, animals, and plants must therefore be treated and cared for as one cares for self.
5. Recognition that every action has an equal and opposite reaction, not only in the world of physics but also that of the human community.
6. Acceptance of the finite nature of all human life, meaning that a minute, hour, or day wasted is a minute, hour, or day lost.

Reason & Commonsense

Reason is not a static commodity. It is a dynamic process available to human beings in the consideration of what is real and, as such, demanding of their attention. It is, further, a process that can be used to make choices and decisions based not on raw or unconsidered desire, but on the experiences of the individual and his or her community of trust. Reason involves seeing the world as it is, not as one wishes it might be or as the various myths common to the human imagination view it. The employment of reason requires not what some religious systems call "faith," but, rather courage—the courage to acknowledge the apparent facts of a matter and to work from there in dealing with them, to work to change for the better what can be changed for the better and to accept what cannot.

Robert and Rachel are happily married and have been for nineteen years. They enjoy a good life due to Robert's income as a successful lawyer and Rachel's as a part-time teacher. Their two children are well-adjusted, do well in school, and enjoy being with Mom and Dad when they are not with friends. You might say theirs is a wonderful life. But then it is discovered that Rachel has a somewhat advanced case of breast cancer that requires surgery, radiation, and chemotherapy. Her doctors are honest in saying that the indicated course of treatment has no guarantee of success. The unspoken counsel is to prepare for the worst.

Once shock and fear have subsided a bit, Robert and Rachel reach out to their parents and a couple of friends, one of whom promises to pray for Rachel and declares that the god she prays to is a good and loving god who wills that no one as good as Rachel should die of this disease. Under no circumstances, the friend says, should they tell their children or anyone of the doctors' "pessimism." The couple is at first heartened by the friend's outlook but then begin to realize what it is. Robert describes it, somewhat inaptly, as "whistling by the graveyard." Together Robert and Rachel decide to face the facts, level with themselves and their children, and proceed with the advised treatment—but to plan for the clear possibility that it will not cure her. They privately discuss how the disfigurement that will be the result of her mastectomy may affect their sex life. They cry; they remember early and comparatively carefree times in their lives, and finally decide to take the kids out to dinner and a show. Next day, they sit down with their children and tell them the facts as simply and as calmly as possible. Everyone sheds tears and confesses fear of what may happen. Robert takes the lead in encouraging all of them to cherish the times they are having and to hope for the best while being prepared for the worst. He had been advised by almost everybody he knew not openly to acknowledge "the worst." He decided that it was best in every way he could think of to face the facts as he knew them and adopt a Plan A/Plan B kind of approach.

Rachel did have a double mastectomy, did have radiation and chemotherapy, suffered quite a bit, lost her hair, and did not respond well to radiation. She never wanted for care and support from Robert and her children, but, in the end, she succumbed. As her family witnessed her descent toward death, they were not surprised or overwhelmed because they had acknowledged in the first place that such was a clear possibility.

In the immediate aftermath of Rachel's death, the friend who had offered to pray for her told Robert and the children that "everything happens for a reason" and that what had happened was the will of God. Robert rejected both ideas and said as much to the well-meaning friend. Robert later said that in doing so, both he and his children found strength in themselves because, as he told another friend, they had been honest with each other from the beginning and did not indulge in false optimism.

Did Rachel's sickness and death hurt Robert and his children? Certainly. Did it all make them sad? To be sure. But somehow they were able in due course to see it all in big-picture fashion. They knew that cancer in all its forms was prevalent, that tens of thousands of people are diagnosed with one variation or another of it every day, and that that random nature of its onset in many cases is a yet-unsolved mystery.

Robert's son, who turned thirteen between his mother's diagnosis and death, went to a novelty shop in the neighborhood mall and made for himself a T-shirt with the slogan SHIT HAPPENS on the front and back. Robert was at first taken aback by it until he realized what his son was saying; then he knew the boy was coping successfully with his abysmal loss.

Considered Experience

A child who is intellectually and mentally well within the normal range sees at just about eye level an object consisting of concentric circles glowing in red, his favorite color. Despite being told many times about touching the stove, he is overcome with curiosity and puts out his hand to touch the object... and screams in pain. His injury is later treated by a physician. He recovers, but will bear for the rest of his life a scar from the incident. It was his experience rather than the parental admonition not to touch the stove that told him the wisdom of not doing so. He never again put his hand on the burner of a stove—hot or cold.

At the dawn of the agricultural revolution, a tribe of several families was led to settle near a river that was said by the tribal elders to be the seat of power of a deity who gave the gift of water to those who worshipped him. The idea was that the closer to the river's edge one built the family shelter and sowed the seed, the richer would be the harvest. In short order, the river flooded its banks and carried away the tribe's ramshackle shelters, their planted seed, and some of their young. Under direction from its elders, the tribe rebuilt and re-sowed in the same places because the river god so demanded. In due time came another flood. This time, one of the tribal members refused to rebuild or to replant at the river's edge, moving himself and his family to higher ground. He was condemned by the tribal elders for his apostasy, but when the rainy season inevitably brought the next flood, he laughed from his promontory and harvested his crop. He and his sons and grandsons prospered as a tribe unto themselves as they acted on experience rather than the myth of the river god.

Dignity & the Human Genome

It is a fact that every living human being and every dead one whose corpse can be analyzed is possessed of the same genome—the sequence of genes on twenty-three chromosome pairs. Sitting Bull was so equipped, as was General George Custer. Adolf Hitler and Anne Frank had the same genome. The same was true of Bull Connor and Martin Luther King, Jr.; Malcom X and Ayn Rand; Harry Houdini and Mark Twain; Czar Nicholas II and Lenin; Emperor Hirohito and General MacArthur; Sigmund Freud and Karl Jung; Wolfgang Amadeus Mozart and Louis Armstrong. The same is true of a gay man and a lesbian, a bisexual and a transsexual person, a homeless street person and the president of General Motors. Rodney King once asked on national television, "People, I just want to say, you know, can we all get along?"

The question was, in fact, a plea—a plea to overcome the racial bias of which King and countless other persons of color were victims. Almost exactly fifty years before King's brutal beating by white Los Angeles police officers, the United States government suddenly and deliberately interned thousands of Japanese Americans in rude camps in the interior West for no other reason than the paranoid suspicion that they had aided and abetted the Japanese navy's attack on Pearl Harbor or would aid and abet further attacks along the American West Coast.

Only eighty years before the internment of the Japanese Americans, the state of South Carolina seceded from the Union over the issue of slavery, and forthwith initiated the ruinous War Between the States. At issue was the right of white people to enslave black people against their will in order to keep an economy afloat. It has been 150 years since the Battle of Fort Sumter, yet many descendants of former slaves live in abject poverty in the ruins of America's inner cities. More than forty-five years after the civil rights legislation of the mid-1960s, they still find themselves victims of poor schools, substandard housing, and marginal employment. The color of their skins and their telltale facial features make the difference.

At the beginning of the second decade of the twenty-first century, gay and lesbian Americans are made to struggle for the right to marry, bequeath to, and inherit from one another, and to enjoy benefits and privileges extended automatically to heterosexual couples. Gay men are easily called "fags" and lesbians "dykes." Society, too often backed up by judicial systems, systematically denies them basic civil rights. The U.S. military continues to struggle with the "don't-ask-don't-tell" policy, with the result that many a capable and brave soldier, seaman, and pilot has been discharged. It isn't the color of their skins or any telltale facial feature that makes the difference for such human beings. It's their natural inclination to seek conjugal love with a person of the same sex.

Racial, social, cultural, economic, and sexual differences in human beings do not affect the nature of the genome of which each and all are the product. Rodney King's rhetorical question as to whether or not we can get along echoes down the corridor of the years as a desperate cry for help. Thus the process of becoming human entails the respect of self and other human beings regardless of the differences that distinguish one from the other. We are not human in any full sense of the word when respect for individual dignity is not a reality.

The baptismal rite of the Episcopal Church in the United States of America has for almost half a century included among the vows that sponsors or adult candidates are required to take as a condition of their baptism this promise: "Will you strive for justice and peace among all people, and respect the dignity of every human being?"[2] At the time the rite was still experimental, the church was riven by conflict over whether the physical and emotional dispositions of women did or did not disqualify them from being ordained as priests. The conflict persisted well into the time when use of the rite had been approved. The church has since suffered schism as a result. For the past forty years, the church has suffered serious conflict and further schism over the ordination of gay and lesbian persons. So much for respecting the dignity of every human being.

Thus even the Episcopal Church is obviously still struggling to become human—a church whose ministers are obliged to proclaim that divinity became human through a first-century CE supernatural virgin birth and that, therefore, the child, while human, was "without sin"—meaning that he could not have been truly human. The ethical wisdom attributed to the adult who had been that child suggests what being human is: turning the other cheek to the smiter, forgiving him as often as necessary, and loving him even if he has declared himself an enemy. It is easy to see why the human race still has a long way to go before becoming fully human.

Care of the Earth, "Our Island Home"[3]

It should seem obvious that the biosphere known as Earth is undergoing rather rapid change for its size and age. Things should by rights be moving, one might say, more glacially. Yet the pace of the change is more and more obvious, as can be seen in the rising sea levels in Pacific Rim island nations, the prolonged droughts in the midsection of North America and in sub-Saharan Africa. Those together with the recent flooding in Pakistan and in Australia, the prolonged hot and cold spells, the melting of polar icecaps and interior glaciers, the ever-increasing parts-per-million carbon dioxide count—all are worrisome reminders that the planet inherited by twentieth- and twenty-first-century earthlings is in distress. The northern migration of various animals and reptiles from the subtropical zones into the temperate zones and the concomitant dying off of certain trees and shrubs that once flourished in those latter zones are proof positive that the planet is warming.

Despite years and years of hard-core scientific investigation and experiment and the observations and recommendations that resulted, two things have become evident: (1) Most people don't seem to care enough to change their habits, and (2) the political class has placed itself in a position of strategic denial of the facts. Aside from psychotic nihilists, one would think, virtually every human being once sufficiently informed of the facts surely would want to do his or her part to maintain and preserve the quality of the environment. The reality is that the political deniers are in league with industrialists in blind pursuit of profit, who devoutly wish to suppress the not-difficult-to-understand information about global warming and climate change. They have co-opted the evangelical clergy for theological support. Many of the eighty-seven new members of the 112th Congress, sent there by the tea party, made plain even before being sworn in that they would vigorously oppose any so-called "job-killing, business-killing" environmental legislation, that they would labor night and day to lift "profit-killing" regulations from mining and manufacturing companies. A frequent biblical citation heard to justify such legislation is Genesis 8:22: "While the earth remaineth, seedtime and harvest, and cold and heat, and summer and winter, and day and night shall not cease"—that being the post-deluge promise of the gods (note, please, that the Hebrew *elohim* is a plural) to Noah. Indeed, those who take the Bible literally rather than seriously interpret that passage along with Genesis 1:28[4] as permitting the sometimes ruinous advances of humankind that leave the tops of mountains blown off, streams running with toxic tailings from mines, great plains with their grasses pulled up, forests denuded, vast urban areas asphalted into parking lots, and the landscape littered with belching smoke stacks, etc. The more internal combustion engines spewing exhaust, the better. The same for more eight-lane freeways. "Have a little faith," the believers say, "God will provide."

The care of the earth is not a faith-based operation. It's a work project, and it's not getting done.

Saving the World by Works

Demonstrably, Earth is not helpless. It strikes back when it is misused. It may be that *Homo sapiens* is the only species on the planet that does not live in harmony with it. He seems to squat upon it and take not so much what he needs but what he wants from it. He is willing to send into its air or water almost any effluent he finds unpleasant, apparently thinking that once it is out of sight it can be out of mind with its unpleasantness resolved by an act of god. He is willing to use every resource he can lay his hands on and to use it up, moving then on to the next thing. As the late economist Herbert Stein said frequently of the economy, so it can be said of the environment: "If something cannot go on forever, it will stop."

Human abuse of the planet and its resources cannot go on if human beings wish their children's children to enjoy life on it. The planet will be saved not by faith but by works. Immediately at issue is the heat-trapping gas carbon dioxide, which is produced by coal-burning power plants and other smokestack industries and by the exhaust from internal combustion engines. Just behind that is the so-called "oil peak," the point at which irreplaceable fossil fuels are becoming scarcer as time goes on, and which point, according to some scientists, has already been passed.[5] If you doubt that every action has an equal and opposite reaction, just look at the price of crude oil going up and up as its supply becomes scarcer and scarcer.

The sane and rational response to these realities is twofold: (1) to reduce consumption of fossil fuels, and (2) to support and encourage the development and wider usage of renewable energy sources. The electric car now once again making a small, tentative place for itself in the showrooms of American auto dealers is one answer. The political will to invest national resources more heavily into attractive and dependable mass transportation is another. People will be more likely to abandon their automobiles for mass transportation, at least for daily use, only when the latter ceases to be a neglected and ramshackle system plagued by unexplainable delays and shoddy equipment.

In a nation that has long since adopted the free-market system, it will take committed individuals and communities to insist on cleaner fuels used by fewer means of transportation. It will also require a change of attitude. The automobile, by its very name, suggests self-mobilization: Whoever has use of an automobile is free or freer to come and go pretty much at will and to make as many trips as he pleases from point A to point B. The more expensive gasoline becomes at the pump, the more often most people will reduce the frequency and length of such trips because income is not infinite. Again, as Stein said, "If something can't go on forever, it will stop." If people decide they want to make a process or a system stop, they will do so and thus create a market for another process or another system. That's basically what happened in the second, third, and fourth decades of the twentieth century, when the automobile went from being an exquisitely crafted toy for millionaires to a mass-produced utilitarian vehicle for everybody else. Eventually, streetcar lines disappeared from cities all over America. In due course, it was only those who could not afford an automobile who had to take the bus. More and more that meant the poor, and fuel-efficient public transportation became a last-resort option.

The automobile industry and the superhighways of the late twentieth century didn't just happen. No invisible hand or deity revealed or instituted them. They were brought about by human beings exercising their entrepreneurial technology to make money. And money they made. Now it is time for another entrepreneurial revolution, because what is happening now cannot go on forever. If Stein is right, it won't. Faith in providence will neither make the floods abate nor the droughts go away, nor yet prevent the tropics from creeping northward. Only the will and the works of intentional human beings can make that happen.

Wind turbines and solar panels are clearly among the answers to the problems caused by the use of fossil fuels. County commissions and township boards along Lake Michigan's eastern shore in Mason and Oceana counties have declined permission for the former as being unsightly. Zoning authorities, for example in Bethesda, Maryland, told *The New York Times* Washington columnist, Thomas Friedman, that his newly installed solar panels were "against the law. Too unsightly."[6] Those who have cast their lot with renewable energy sources are often considered nonconformist hippies and are subject to the kind of suspicion that people with long hair and beads used to have to tolerate. Just as the bus systems in many cities are seen as transportation for the poor, so wind turbines and solar panels are seen as far-out and weird intrusions on an established landscape. However, when the costs of generating electricity and its retail distribution have so increased as to be ruinous, those who once resented wind turbines and solar panels on aesthetic grounds will embrace them, and those devices will become more and more popular. As gasoline prices increase beyond the stagnant wages of the middle class, urban populations will begin to return more and more to using mass transit. When—or if—that happens, the efficiency of those systems will increase at least to adequate levels. The effect of no occult hand will be felt in any of this. It will come about through the combined power of human ingenuity and human demand. If the market fails to respond in acceptable ways to demand, an armed revolution may eventually be mounted against the "malefactors of great wealth."[7] Faith without works is not only dead but deadly.

Now in the Time of This Mortal Life[8]

When do we begin? How urgent is the situation? Can't we wait and see if enough people buy electric cars? I think I'll wait until they're cheaper. I can't afford to put more insulation in my house, but I have to have it at least 72 degrees inside summer and winter. Such are thoughts that pass through the minds of most of us in the American middle class. We're well enough off to afford to heat and cool our homes, though maybe just barely so. And we have become accustomed to paying more than three dollars per gallon for gasoline. The decline in the quality and availability of dependable public transportation has driven us, literally, to our cars. We know that personal reform along these lines must be now or never, but we also know that it cannot be now.

Such is the conundrum that bedevils us in 2012. Any rational person knows there is no messiah in the wings who will come to save us and the world from the disaster toward the onset of which we creep day by day. At first it will be an economic one as the weather patterns worsen due to global warming and climate change. The cost of food and fuel will outpace average incomes, to say nothing of those of people at the bottom of the economic heap. The affluent will hunker down behind the guardhouses of their gated communities. Gasoline stations and grocery stores will become venues of violence as people who come with their money to buy what they need are assaulted and robbed by people who have no money to buy what they need. Think of an American Somalia. The various levels of government and their police forces will either respond to the commands of the affluent to put down the beginnings of revolution, or they will eventually join the mob as chaos becomes the norm. Preposterous, you say?

Fewer than one hundred years ago, just such a thing occurred in Russia as the Bolsheviks won the day against the Czarists and attempted to redress centuries' worth of political, economic and social grievances. The revolution was seriously bungled, and it took more than seventy years for it to fall apart completely. The system based on faith in Mother Russia, its divinely enthroned czar, and its church had failed catastrophically. The revolution was the work of flawed but determined men. Its undoing was likewise the work of determined and flawed men and women. Even a cursory reading of Russian history from 1870 to 1917 demonstrates that none of the monumental suffering that the revolution brought and none of the unconscionable deprivation that the poor and disadvantaged had suffered for centuries before was inevitable. At almost any time until February or March 1917, the tide was reversible. Those in power knew that things had to change. They knew it had to be now or never, but they knew it could not be now.

That kind of fatal knowledge proceeds from the minds of not-yet-human beings. Those who are truly human always know what time it is and what the present time demands. They work day and night to make happen whatever needs to happen. They know deep within that a current moment may be the last moment in which they can speak or act effectively to save themselves and others from failure or catastrophe. They know that "now" is always the time. They know that salvation always comes of works, not of faith. They know that what people glibly refer to as "faith" is in reality no more and no less than courage—the courage to be actors rather than the acted upon, the courage to do what needs to be done for salvation's sake.

Notes

1. Donne, *Nunc lento sonitu dicunt, morieris*, pp. 106–7 in *Devotions*.
2. *The Book of Common Prayer*, 1979, 305.
3. *The Book of Common Prayer*, 1979, 370.
4. "The gods said unto them, 'Be fruitful and multiply, and replenish the earth and subdue it; and have dominion over . . . every living thing that moveth upon the earth.'"
5. Jeremy Hsu in a LiveScience article of March 12, 2010, quotes Kuwait University and Swedish scientists saying that the oil production peak will be reached as early as 2014 and no later than 2018.

6. Friedman, *Hot, Flat, And Crowded*, 2008, pp. 206–7.
7. A phrase coined and first used by President Theodore Roosevelt in a 1907 speech at Provincetown, MA.
8. *The Book of Common Prayer*, 1928, 90.

CHAPTER

12

Negotiating Life as a Humanist

Conventional religion and social custom do not easily admit of the existence of humanists or of the acceptability of humanism. The avowed humanist might as well have a wind turbine and solar panels and be off the electrical grid for all the respect he will get from his conformist neighbors. The nonconformist is always slightly under suspicion. All the more so when his nonconformity extends to religion. Humanism has been a major target of the evangelical Right since the latter's renascence in the late 1970s. Humanists did not belong to or attend churches and, except for a relatively few humanist Jews, did not belong to synagogues. Humanists in the 1970s and '80s were the suspected communists of the late 1940s and early '50s. Why?

The humanist does not look to an unseen and unknown deity for meaning or authority. The humanist looks to himself or herself and the community of humankind for meaning and authority. The humanist's entire focus is on the well-being of his or her fellow human beings and, of course, on the state of the environment—natural, social, political, economical—in which they live and have their being. These people and their situation the humanist can see and hear. Direct communication with them for the purpose of knowing them, their needs, and their aspirations is a supplemental aim; a community self-empowered to share resources and pursue the realization of aspirations is the desired end. Instead of praying to an unseen deity whose existence no amount of theological wizardry can prove, humanists make their wishes known to one another and hope to find mutuality in those aspirations and the self-generated power to achieve them. The humanist does not argue with the theist about whether the theist's god is real or imagined. Live and let live is the idea here, but the humanist deals with the data that his senses, experience, and reason try to sort out. If a god there be, fine. But until the data to support that idea become apparent, the humanist says "No thanks."

That's because the humanist is an avowed agnostic, that is, he or she "does not know"—does not know enough due to the absence of reliable data enabling a reasonable person to posit the existence or reality of an unseen deity. The humanist is also not a deist nor yet a pantheist—just an agnostic, willing to assert neither that there is a god nor that there isn't, inasmuch as insufficient data are available to say otherwise. In that respect, humanists tend to embrace the scientific method and the work that flows from its practice. The emergence of a credible hypothesis arising out of data, the gathering of further relevant data, and the testing of the hypothesis against the data may or may not yield a credible explanation for whatever is being studied. The scientist keeps on testing until, as happens in rare instances, the hypothesis is received by the scientific community as a full-fledged Theory, and thus accepted as the most reasonable and likely explanation for the phenomena under consideration. It never becomes a settled thing, since new data are bound to show up, and therefore the matter is left in a conditional or contingent state pending further research. Agnosticism is an important aspect of such a process.

Finally, the humanist is of a secular disposition—meaning only that he or she is concerned for the here-and-now inasmuch as any then-and-there is the province of religious speculation. The humanist embraces the world (which is what the adjective "secular" connotes) and operates within it in the time frame available. The idea is to leave the world in as good or better state than it was found. Such work involves the expression of selfless love in human relationships; efforts to seek inward and outward beauty in people, places, things, and events; and the celebration of life as an amazing opportunity to experience the world's light, color, texture, sounds, tastes, and smells. And some of these are natural, while others are of human provenance—all the way from the uplifting harmonies of the Bach B Minor Mass to the aroma of a loaf of baking bread, from the sound of a happy child's voice to the promontory of a far mountain range bathed in the light of a setting sun.

The humanist is concerned with feeding the hungry, providing shelter to the homeless, medical care to the needy, and other material and emotional support to the disadvantaged. Why? Because they are human beings with the same genome as the humanist, and with the same potential and possibility as he or she. To the humanist, no individual life is unimportant, no community of individuals insignificant. Humanist Rabbi Tamara Kolton put it this way in a visit with a confirmation class from an Episcopal Church: "We're all we have, together and individually. And the fewer lines we draw to separate ourselves from each other, the more we realize that what we are is human.

That's our main identity. After that comes anything else we may be or call ourselves."[1]

Humanists believe in themselves, but never exclusively in themselves as individuals; for they know they are but members of the human family in its present existence, and as such feel obliged to do what they can to bequeath to future generations a better world than they found.

It's as simple as Hillel the Elder and Jesus of Nazareth are said to have explained. Hillel: "What you hate, do not do to another." Jesus: "Do to others as you would have done to yourself." Humanism is both self- and other-centered. As Jesus of Nazareth was said to have advised: "Love your neighbor as yourself."

Notes

1. Kolton now leads the Birmingham Temple in Farmington Hills, MI, in which secular humanist Judaism had its beginnings under the late Rabbi Sherwin T. Wine (1928–2007).

CHAPTER 13

Practical Considerations

Agnostic secular humanism is never found in its pure state. It is neither absolute nor constant. Plenty of families who are not conventionally religious put up Christmas trees and sing Christmas carols. A sudden shift from a vague, generic religiosity to a well-defined secular humanism or to an over-the-top theism is seldom the norm. Abrupt conversions from one extreme to another are not to be trusted. One's take on life and the world is a continuum along which one moves to and fro on the axes of knowledge and feeling. Healthy skepticism is an appropriate response to absolutist assertions. A willingness to consider a conditional or contingent proposition is likewise a decent response. Living with and into well-thought-out approaches to unresolved issues requires the agnostic secular humanist to resist final answers, especially when they partake in any vague and pious there-and-then-isms and when they deal with abstractions rather than with the welfare of human beings and their environment. This rubric can and should be applied to economics and politics.

Too often, both economics and politics operate on such abstract principles as "democracy is the highest and best form of governance, even (some insist) the will of God for human beings" or "the free-market system is the best economic model," or "little or no taxation is the ideal arrangement," or "welfare for the poor via taxation on the rich is larceny." The humanist will invariably want to know how any policy that proceeds from any airy principle will affect the lives of any human beings, especially those human beings who possess and control a very sparse share of the world's goods. The humanist will strike that attitude because he or she cares first and foremost for human beings in the here-and-now. The humanist will likewise insist that people come before principle, that "now" must be dealt with before "then," and that policies cannot be pursued merely on assertions of their correctness or singular effectiveness.

If humanism must be categorized, then call it "pragmatic ethics." Humanists prefer those principles-become-policies that promise better outcomes for people, even sometimes the greatest good for the greatest number with allowances made for those represented in the lesser number—this because the humanist cannot be a perfectionist or agree to allow the best to be the enemy of the better.

Ultimately, humanism is a work in progress. The humanist does not stand with arms at the side waiting for some external agency to present solutions and answers as if they were rabbits plucked from a magician's hat. The New Testament Greek word ἐργον—*ergon*—means "work." The word is used to account for such phenomena as the cleansing of the lepers or the restoration of sight to the blind. Today such events are carelessly called "miracles," but in the gospels, the label for such a deed is *ergon*—reflecting, no doubt, that in the world of physics an *erg* is a unit of work, what we nonphysicists might call an applied force or effort. Things happen as a result of work done.

The central idea of this book is that whatever salvation human beings seek must needs be sought in and for the here-and-now, within and for themselves in community and in their unselfish pursuit of happiness. That salvation comes by and through works to which human beings apply themselves actively, rather than passively awaiting it to dawn upon them simply because they have been taught to believe it will if only they have faith.

In a passage from 1 Corinthians, Paul, the Jew, used this phrase: "The message about the cross...."[1] Paul said it was one thing to one type of person, and another to a different type. But what is "the message about the cross"? It is that sometimes it takes a life laid down to accomplish selfless works of necessity. It is not what happened on the cross that saves us, for that death of a martyr to a cause is variously depicted in the mythologies of the New Testament gospels. Salvation occurs only to the degree that people of whatever religious commitment, or of no religious commitment, emulate that extreme model of love-laid-down kind of sacrifice. Mohandas Gandhi and Martin Luther King, Jr., followed in that train just as surely as their persistence in speaking truth to power and their demands that justice be done led directly to their assassinations.

Whatever salvation means—from what or for what—its pursuit must come through works performed by human beings who understand that such works constitute the compelling agenda for the here-and-now. The most effective way to pursue it is one day at a time, one step at a time, lived and walked with courage, and acknowledging that "the meaningful life is not to get rid of problems. It is to live with them, confront them, and sometimes win."[2]

Notes

1. 1:18 (NRSV).
2. Wine, *Staying Sane in a Crazy World*, 119.

CHAPTER 14

A Sermon for Would-Be Humanists[1]

On February 12, 1809, two infant boys were spending their first full day of life outside the womb. One was undoubtedly in the care of his nurse in the pleasant English village of Shrewsbury, Shropshire; the other of his mother in a primitive backwoods cottage in rural Kentucky. The first was Charles Robert Darwin. The second was Abraham Lincoln. Who could have known on that day a little over two centuries ago how much each of those infants would bequeath to the human race? Of Darwin, perhaps, more might have been expected than of Lincoln, due to the circumstances of their births—due also, as time went on, to their divergent opportunities. Darwin was university-educated; Lincoln was mostly an autodidact. The former surely knew of and read about the latter, but it is doubtful that Lincoln had either the time or the opportunity to read *The Origin of Species,* since it was published a year before his election as president of the United States and the days, weeks, and months of his first term were overborne with crises of secession, war, and political backbiting.

In addition to being born on the same date, Darwin and Lincoln had in common the propensity to inquire. *Inquiry* is my middle name; that is, I am firmly convinced that religion of the only kind I can tolerate is all about inquiry. It's all about the question, about formulating the question, refining it, researching the data that prompted the question in the first place, analyzing the fruits of that research. Still, the primary goal is not always to wrest an answer from these efforts, but often to enable further consideration and formulation of the question itself.

The word "inquiry" occurred prominently in the titles of my last two books.[2] In fact, "inquiry" properly occupies a central role in the life of any scholar. Religion of the organized kind has always seemed to me to be far more about answers than questions. I used to say of the congregation I served for twenty-two years that our church was "a center for critical thinking and evolving belief."

It was an Episcopal Church where that kind of concept was not universally appreciated. I shrink from creeds, especially the two that appear in *The Book of Common Prayer*. The first was formulated as early as the second century of the Common Era, the second by a convocation of largely clueless bishops assembled by Constantine the Great circa 330 CE to settle the burning question of whether the Son (uppercase "S") was of the same or of a similar substance as the Father (uppercase "F"). In the sixteen hundred years since that latter creed was wrought from less than the noblest of political considerations, Christian belief has evolved with dissidents anathematized and conformity coerced.[3]

Belief is still evolving whether the theologians like it or not. Some people are evolving right out of the belief business both wholesale and retail. Over the years, many people in one way or another have said, "I'm trying to figure out what to believe." I always say in response, "Me, too. Looks like you've come to the right place."

A good many churches exist to provide answers and, often enough, to stifle inquiry. What if Charles Darwin had been content with the certainties of his nineteenth-century

Anglican faith and its dependence on the Bible for settled truth? What if he had not asked and pondered the questions his observations raised in his fertile mind? What if he had not dwelt on the behavior and appearances of the tortoises off Galapagos? Imagine how badly off the biosciences would be but for Darwin's epoch-making work. He didn't get there by grasping for answers. He got there by honoring at every stage the question and never really letting go of inquiry.

Darwin's contemporary, Abraham Lincoln, certainly must have engaged in a great deal of internal inquiry. The Great Emancipator did not come to office with the intention of emancipating any single person or class of people. He came, as it turned out, to preserve the Union, and for some time believed members of the black race to be inferior to their white counterparts. Lincoln thought the kindest thing might be to relocate them all to Africa. Imagine where this country would be today if Lincoln had stopped with those half-baked thoughts, stopped asking and inquiring of himself and others if such propositions made sense. They did not, of course, and Lincoln found that out by pressing his inquiry.

Darwin was vilified for the results of his inquiry as expressed in *The Origin of Species.* Lincoln was assassinated for the results of his. Darwin's eventual observations and Lincoln's Emancipation Proclamation with his embrace of racial equality have survived to change the direction of the world. It was inquiry and the evolution of thought that brought about those epoch-making changes.

Darwin's observations and conditional conclusions may seem elementary from the vantage point of the year 2011, but in 1859, the idea that all life forms evolved from a common ancestor was both fabulous and fabulously threatening, not to mention in opposition to the Holy Bible. The idea that only the fit survive was obnoxious to those who believed and believe that the future, both in general and in particular as concerns individuals, is in the hands of an omnipotent and omniscient deity.

We can thank Albert Einstein and his generation of geniuses for helping us start to begin to commence to grasp the vastness of the universe and its puzzling characteristic of relativity. One has to bend oneself into a mental pretzel to make room for the uncritical idea of how the biblical god could fit into that portrait of reality.

Because conventional religion is as often as not reactionary, inquiry is thought to verge on heresy. Such an attitude aids and abets the hardening of communal arteries, and proclamation takes the place of inquiry. At that point, inquiry stops and a hardening of the communal arteries sets in. Rearview-mirror stasis replaces forward-looking possibilities. That, coupled with high-volume certitude, tends to shut down inquiry. What makes us quintessentially human is the capacity to inquire.

Conventional religious belief and practice are generally a drag on society and tend to form roadblocks to progressive education. For example, even in the second decade of the twenty-first century, public school boards throughout the country continued to be pressed by the Christian Right to teach creationism or intelligent design in addition to or in place of evolutionary biology. In an article dated January 28, 2011, Science magazine tells an alarming story: 60 percent of public school science teachers are afraid to teach the Theory of Natural Selection for fear of community criticism. About 20 percent of high school biology teachers make no bones about out-and-out teaching creationism. In what is widely considered the most advanced nation on the planet, many forces act counter to that advancement—forces that, if they were to prevail, would set us back seriously. In defense of static, don't-ask-any-questions dogma, they would rob women of their reproductive rights and make a whole generation of children ignorant and useless as contributing adults.

Yet when people are involved in inquiry, rather than proclamation, the world is safer.

To stimulate inquiry, one might read and recommend to others Mark Hertsgaard's *Hot: Living Through the Next 50 Years on Earth* (2011). Hertsgaard would, of course, be dismissed as hysterical by the climate-change deniers—who may as well be called "holocaust deniers," given what Hertsgaard demonstrates in his fact-laden, no holds barred forecast of what has already begun to happen on this planet of ours. We are in for massive droughts, the catastrophic rise of sea levels, and unprecedented famine—all because the developed nations cannot and will not curb their addiction to fossil fuels. Hertsgaard despairs of the climate-change deniers and their smug piety about a God who has everything under control if we would only trust Him.

What we have to do is to stamp out that antique philosophy of religion that clings to belief in the beneficence of an omnipotent deity who can be petitioned through prayer to stay the floodwaters or make it rain or to do whatever else our hearts may desire. The politest word to describe that form of self-delusion is *baloney*.

There is no deity that will save us. We will save ourselves—or not. And this goes directly to the question posed by a protestor in Tahrir Square in Cairo on the world-shaking occasion in February 2011 when a peaceful demonstration brought down a strong-man president and his government: "How do you build a secular, modern state for religious people?"

The first thing you do is to remove from governing principles all *a priori* assumptions not supported by objective data and rely instead on experience and reason. Inevitably, any rigid dogma arising from *a priori* assumptions that demand conformity will be in conflict with other such convictions and beliefs, and that conflict will ignite the kind of ruinous strife that we see, for example, in Iraq between rival Islamic sects.

Events have moved me often to think that religion may be the death of us all—that is, if religion in the end abandons inquiry for unbending certitude, and reason for blind faith.

Human beings not only do not know enough to posit the existence of omnipotent and omniscient deities. It is a fact that we do not know what we do not know. Nor should we expect that any amount of inquiry, however rigorous, will yield such knowledge. As the psalmist said, "Such knowledge is too wonderful and excellent for me; I cannot attain unto it."[4]

Inquiry, then, is a work of the humble striver like Darwin, who took twenty-two years to formulate and publish his remarkable findings, and then only with great hesitation. He did not trumpet his work, but offered it for the consideration of thoughtful persons who might be ready and able to see things as he saw them.

Notes

1. Given by the author on February 13, 2011, at C3 Exchange, An Inclusive Spiritual Community, Spring Lake, MI.
2. *Asking: Inquirers in Conversation,* 2010, and *Resonance: Biblical Texts Speaking to 21st Century Inquirers,* 2011.
3. See Cook, *Christianity Beyond Creeds.*
4. Psalm 139:5, *The Book of Common Prayer,* 1928, 514.

Epilogue

Humanism, especially because of its secular agnostic orientation, can be and often is threatening to those whose socioreligious orientation tends to the uncritical and conventional. Yet over my forty-five years as a leader of three different congregations (rural, urban, and suburban) and as a humanist, I found it both possible and helpful to preach and teach out of the accepted canonical texts of the Bible based on research conducted according to academic canons. I employed the fruits of that research to texts in ways that the language I used and the concepts to which I alluded were reasonably within the comfort zone of those congregations, and at the same time did not cause me to be intellectually dishonest. I did not always manage to avoid conflict, especially with the more rigidly orthodox, yet I did inspire a great many people to take a second look at their unexamined assumptions about religion in general and biblical language in particular. I thus proved, at least to myself, that an agnostic secular humanist can speak to self-consciously religious people and be heard, sometimes with pretty good results. I proved—again, to myself—that parish ministers can be working scholars and preach and teach out of that scholarship. I believe that kind of work will be the salvation of the Judeo-Christian experience or of any religious experience. At the very least, it will save from irrelevance those people who embrace its rigors, and will enable their institutions and movements to engage in the vital work of solving both material and intellectual human problems, rather than to be part of that which needs solving.

The practical application of that work is moving to action people who have been engaged in thinking and reflection. If what religious communities have been doing has not measurably improved the environment in which they have been doing it, they should stop doing whatever that is and do something different. Getting some positive thing done effectively is the final measure of relevance insofar as the humanist is concerned.

Even as this epilogue is being composed, the Republicans in the 112th Congress are, in effect, offering an opportunity for synagogue, church, mosque, and temple congregations to return to relevance: for example, they are engaged in hell-bent legislative efforts to dismantle the Head Start program and to annihilate Planned Parenthood—all for the purpose of redistributing wealth from the lower and middle classes to the corporate upper class. The reformers say of their desire to defund early education programs that moms should just stay home and take care of their children rather than go out to work, regardless of the financial hardship that would ensue. Of Planned Parenthood, the crusaders say that reproductive rights are nonexistent.

It may be that the self-styled fiscal conservatives will achieve some or even all of what they have set out to do. If so, something would have to be done to replace the vital services that Head Start and Planned Parenthood have provided. If religious communities can run food pantries and soup kitchens, they ought to be able to replicate at the local level some semblance of the critical services those two programs offer. I am not so naïve as to think that Roman Catholic parishes would be setting up shop to dispense contraceptive advice or contraceptives themselves, much less to help women understand what their constitutionally protected reproductive rights are, but certainly any congregation can do something about providing educational offerings. This I know from personal experience.

In the early 1970s—at about the time my inner-city Detroit congregation was looking for some good to do—there began what would turn out to be a two-month long labor-management standoff between the city's Board of Education and its corps of teachers. On the day after Labor Day, the schools did not open, and it became pretty clear that they would remain closed indefinitely. One of the locked-out teachers, a member of the congregation, came to me with the idea of opening a free school using every square foot of our modest buildings. I was right there with him but doubted we could pull it off. "We have to get these kids off the street and back into learning," he insisted. Forthwith, he recruited about a dozen of his jobless colleagues, and the Emmanuel Church and Community House Free School was open for business. Word of its availability spilled onto the street, and by the second day we were at capacity. It was not a baby-sitting enterprise but a real school. I even taught an English class and managed to introduce a dozen or so initially bored teenagers to Keats and Shelley.

If a fair contract had not been achieved and approved by the city's teachers, I suppose we could have continued for the rest of the year, and maybe even into the next. I was even planning in my head what I would teach in a second semester. *Beowulf?* Probably not. I thought of *The Catcher in the Rye*. That might have worked out. Had we gone on for much longer than we did, I would have felt compelled to quit the classroom for the fundraising trail to provide at least some minimal income for those who were teaching for free. Toward the end of October, though, they were back in their own classrooms, and the free school became part of the congregation's proud history of making a positive difference. Several children from the neighborhood begged parents to let them come to Emmanuel instead of going to their assigned school.

Those of the congregation who turned out to help with the free school learned an important lesson about the power for good inherent in the institutions of religion: namely, that they can respond handily to crises in the public sector by doing what the public sector cannot or will not do. My dirt-poor seventy-five-family inner-city church, already trying simply to survive, was able to get up and running a K-12 school that lasted for nearly eight weeks, then followed that up with a permanent preschool program, which, for all I know, may still be intact. I have been told by my elitist liberal acquaintances that stepping in to do the public sector's work only enables its neglect and desire to direct its resources upward along the food chain. True enough, but there remain children to be educated, and they cannot be held hostage to a philosophical dispute.

Meanwhile, it is said that a Galilean Jew named Jesus told the members of his hometown *shul* that they ought to emulate Isaiah, the prophet of old, who proclaimed good news to the poor and liberty to the captives.[1] It is said that Jesus was nearly lynched for his trouble, but nobody appeared to question the immediate relevance of his advocacy. The story is that he went on pressing that relevance until it became a mortal threat to the religious, political, and economic establishments. Executed for the crime of advocating relevance, he was later joined in the human pantheon of martyrs by such giants of morality as Mohandas Gandhi and Martin Luther King, Jr., Should twenty-first century religious communities follow them as exemplars, they may be able to say as they are being killed, but *Behold, we live....*² The salvific works of Gandhi and King, long dead, live in more than blessed memory.

Notes

1. Luke 4:14–30.
2. 2 Corinthians 6:9 (KJV).

Appendix

Religion and Democracy

An American Experiment[1]

During the winter of 2011, we saw in the resistance and rebellion of Middle Eastern peoples what some perceived as a hunger and thirst for democracy. But what is "democracy"? In its original tongue, the word is made up of *demos*—people, and *kratos*—power or strength. "People power," in other words. A mob, unruly or otherwise, can be "people power." Get enough people in a square or on a street or in a state capitol building, and you have some form of "people power": power simply to make noise and look rowdy, or power to force real change.

How did America attain democracy? The eighteenth century in Western Europe, especially France, was the fullness of the Enlightenment. Bacon, Hume, and Descartes had done their work. The exclamation mark of proclamation had been exchanged for the question mark of inquiry. In such a climate, kings and emperors by divine right were unwelcome, unwanted, and becoming things of the past. One wishes France had not employed the guillotine in the pursuit of democracy. England did it more gradually, building on the promise of Runymede for some 500 years before it arrived at democracy, though the Cromwell years, their onset and denouement, were not pretty. America's path toward democracy was less than ideal as the immigrant citizenry chose to dehumanize native Americans so as to take possession of the soil that would become, as it would be said, the land of the free and the home of the brave.

Much to our good fortune, the Mubaraks and Gadhafis of the eighteenth century lived an ocean away, making the American Revolution a bit easier, though some 34,520 lives were lost in that war by battle and disease among American, British, and Hessian troops. It took about four years after that war was over for the Articles of Confederation to be succeeded by the document that begins with the immortal words, "We the People of the United States, in order to form a more perfect Union...." That document has been hijacked to some extent by political extremists much as fundamentalists have hijacked the Bible. They use it piecemeal, with no background in its history, out of context, and to their own ends, much in the same way they would accuse the so-called Islamo-Fascist of using the Holy Qur'an. It was the clarion call of the Declaration of Independence that laid down the markers for American democracy in these well-known words: "We hold these truths to be self-evident, that all Men are created equal, that they are endowed by their Creator with certain unalienable rights, that among these are Life, Liberty and the Pursuit of Happiness...." Succored by that hope, our founding parents eventually put together piece by piece a constitutional document that would more or less guarantee a government, as Lincoln would later put it, "of the People, by the People and for the People"—not including, however, Native Americans or Africans who had been brought to these shores in chains. Also it must be remembered that women were not among those thought to be created equal with men until the Nineteenth Amendment, Women's Suffrage, was ratified on August 18, 1920, just in time for the election of Warren Harding.

For all of the rote celebration of democracy in which the power of the people is almost entirely focused on the secret ballot, the number of registered voters who bother to cast a ballot in most elections hovers around 60 percent. I would call that a calamity—not because people may be lazy or uncaring, but because they apparently think the individual vote does not count for much. What democracy has come to mean at the street level is that everybody feels entitled to his own opinion, no matter how far from the facts it may be. Everyone seems to think he has the right to do almost anything he desires, and please get out of the way. But that is not what democracy means. Democracy means attaining intellectually and morally the power to create the present and future of a society, a nation. A nation such as the United States of America has become is socially complex and, due to two centuries of immigration, multicultural and religiously pluralistic.

Thus Americans might be well served by asking the following questions of their nation: (1) Is the United States of America a secular nation? (2) What kind of society has been in the building for the 223 years since the ratification of the as-yet-unamended constitution on September 17, 1787? (3) What has been, is, and should be the place of religion in this nation?

First question: Is the United States of America a secular state? What does the word "secular" mean? It is not the opposite of "sacred." "Secular" derives, as do so many important words in our common vocabulary, from Latin. And in that language it means *this world,* or *this present age.* A state or a nation had better be focused on this world, unless its populace thinks it will soon colonize Mars in large numbers. A state or nation had better be focused on the concerns of this present time and age because there is no other time or age with which to be concerned. The word "secular" has been the byword of evangelical fundamentalists who claim that secularism arises from the musings of the fifth-century BCE philosopher Protagoras. "Man is the measure of all things," he said, by which he meant that the value or worth of those things required for human use is measured by how much real value they actually have. Protagoras was not saying that man is the measure of all things seen and unseen.

Who but those of enormous wealth can afford not to be concerned about the price of gasoline at the pump, or the declining value of his home, or his job security or that of his adult children? Is there someone somewhere, excepting those with seemingly endless wealth, who does not worry about the availability of decent health care insurance against the onset of a major illness or the occurrence of a major accident? Doubtful. That makes us a "secular" people—properly concerned with the present troubles and challenges that are sufficient unto the day. Our governments, such as they are, labor (sometimes stupidly or in vain) to deal with the problems and opportunities dead ahead. The United States Senate does not sit in its chamber contemplating ultimate reality. However clumsily it deals with present problems, its members are dealing with a here-and-now. Thus the United States of America and its government are secular in the sense that I have explained. Both were designed to be secular.

Recall the history: Those of our founding parents who can be most credited for the nature and culture of our American government emerged almost entirely from the Continental Enlightenment, intellectually speaking, and late seventeenth-century Anglicanism, religiously speaking. Rethinking, resistance, and revolution were the chief elixirs in the oxygen of that era in Europe and Britain, that is to say among the elite classes. The Anglican religion of the time was high-and-dry. Evangelical enthusiasms were discouraged. Driving that cool-ish attitude toward religion and its observances was the air of inquiry that, for example, the empiricist David Hume brought to the argument. Reason had replaced faith as the method of determining what was real and, therefore, impingent upon human beings and their decision-making process. That air was imbibed by the grandparents and parents of such colonial savants as Thomas Jefferson and James Madison.

As the founders, with the war of revolution decisively won, sat down to figure out how to design the government of their new nation, they decided to avoid on behalf of their own and future generations the kind of religious conflicts that had bedeviled Europe and England for time out of mind. They were allergic to the idea of the divine right of kings and, eventually, to the idea and reality of monarchy. So entwined in a mesh of power and privilege were the English monarchy and its established church that dissent was well nigh impossible in the British Isles. Jefferson and Madison in their own separate ways insisted that the new nation give religion a wide berth and let its various expressions compete with one another for the attention of the populace—but prohibit interference in the work of governance. Thus was the first work of American genius accomplished in these sixteen amazing words: "Congress shall make no law respecting an establishment of religion, or prohibiting the free exercise thereof." That turned out to mean, as President Jefferson told the Baptist ministers of Danbury, Connecticut, in 1802, that state and church needed a wall of separation to keep them out of each other's hair, clearly implying not only the constitutional right of freedom of religion but also, by logical extension, freedom from religion. Call it a pro-choice matter.

The result of our First Amendment toleration of religion has been our becoming the most overtly religious country in the Western world, with churches, synagogues, mosques, and temples on every avenue, street, road, and lane in America—each and all of them off the tax rolls, each and all of them dependent upon local police and fire departments and other public services that they do not support with so much as a dime in property taxes—all making it pretty clear that America is a secular nation that respects the sacred spaces and structures of its religiously oriented people but thanks them for tending to their own concerns and impinging in no way upon the governance of their nonreligious neighbors.

That said, it must be acknowledged that preaching clergy were prominent in the abolition movement of mid-nineteenth-century America. Those clergy must be credited with helping to move Abraham Lincoln away from his idea of deporting black slaves to Africa and toward the Emancipation Proclamation. In no wise can the public witness of such American giants as Martin Luther King, Jr., be forgotten—he who went to the steps of the Lincoln Memorial to deliver his famed "I Have A Dream Speech," in the text of which he quoted the Hebrew bible, saying, "We will not be satisfied until 'justice rolls down like waters, and righteousness like a mighty stream'"[2] and went on to make repeated references to the Jewish-Christian deity, as would any good Baptist preacher. It must finally be acknowledged that Abraham Lincoln's Second Inaugural made extensive use of biblical texts—yet both Lincoln and King employed religious themes and ideas to champion secular, that is to say "here-and-now," necessities and events.

Second question: What kind of society has been in the building for the 223 years since the ratification of the as-yet-unamended constitution? The answer, where the relationship of religion and democracy is concerned, is "a mixed bag." As we have observed, America is not now and never has been a self-consciously a-religious state, and while now and again (mostly lately) its politics and governance have seemed to lean toward religiosity, it remains, if not purely secular, certainly inclined to be secular. Yes, sessions of Congress and the several legislatures are likely to be opened with formal prayers as clergy from up and down the continuum of theologies regularly take to the dais to inform their deity of choice that the honorable senators or representatives are present and accounted for. If the pray-er happens to have internalized his or her particular religion's hunger and thirst for justice, what generally follows in the sausage-making process of legislation turns out to be anything but just. For example, a majority of members of the U.S. House of Representatives voted in February 2011 to defund Planned Parenthood and to turn a couple of hundred thousand poor kids out of Head Start. However, speaking of democracy, it must be acknowledged that voters sent to Congress in November 2010 a rather large number of office-seekers who had made no bones about cutting off government at the knees, no matter what. Those members of Congress did not get there by stealth, though stealth money from exceedingly wealthy people underwrote their campaigns. Yet Mr. and Mrs. Voter were the ones who pulled the levers or filled in the boxes. That's democracy at work—perhaps not an enlightened democracy, but nobody was lurking in the voting booths putting guns to people's heads.

The kind of society that we have built for ourselves is often democratic in name only. The vote is the keystone of the democratic process. Nobody can make one vote for Candidate A or Candidate B, but they can try to persuade a voter in either direction. Voters sometimes cast their ballots, it is said, out of anger about one thing or another, or out of resentment or with vengeance in their hearts. Among the most crucially important things people have the freedom to do in a democracy is to vote. Therefore voting should be done knowingly, soberly, and in keeping with the solemnity of its intended result.

Of late in the nation's bookstores one cannot help but notice the reissued and much-promoted *Rediscovering God in America*.[3] It was written by former Speaker of the House Newt Gingrich. It is neither a theological work nor that of a scholar of religious ideas. It is the title of a campaigner for public office trying to get there by riding a wave of piety. Gingrich's main complaint is that members of an elite class are trying to create a secular America. It's too late for that. Our founding parents created a secular America, but with freedom of and from religion. So to answer the question about what kind of society have we been building, it must be said that we have an as-yet unfinished society constantly being worked over by circumstances, events, political movements, and politicians. This brings us to the *third question:* What has been, is, and should be the place of religion in this nation?

That's really three more questions: What *has been* the position of religion in America? What *is* the position of religion in America? Finally, what *should be* the place of religion in America?

The First Amendment's prohibition against establishment was new under the sun at the end of the eighteenth century and represented a hope as much as a developing reality. Its direct result was over time the emerging of one of the most self-consciously and overtly religious nations ever. Pick up any Yellow Pages directory of churches, synagogues, and mosques in America; and there they are, one after the other, located on land and in edifices that are exempted from property taxes and in which pretty much anything any priest, rabbi, minister, or imam wishes to say may be said — and that with impunity. The archetypal New England village square with town hall at one end, post office and public library at the other, and churches of various denominations set around the sides, is the kind of picture that evolved from the end of the eighteenth century and into the nineteenth. The reverend clergy were generally respected, and in most cases members of their individual flocks went about their religious lives respecting those of others.

The position of religion in American life in the early twenty-first century is in a way exemplified by what one invariably hears as the last words from a president of the United States at the end of any major televised speech: "God bless you and may God bless America." If those eight words were not to be uttered, that would be the news headline, no matter what else the president may have said. The Religious Right would run amok in righteous indignation while unbelievers would for once feel included in the national embrace. The political fact that those words must be said, no matter what the one speaking them actually means, seems to be beside the point.

Sessions of both houses of Congress are convened with prayers by various clergy across a wide spectrum of belief. Presidents generally place a hand on an open Bible as they take the oath of office. But perversely enough, what sometimes issues from the White House or from Congress is anything but respectful of the stated values of most religions, which emphasize the values of peace and justice.

What place *should* religion occupy in a nation founded on secular principles? Any position its local communities and national organizations can attain without interfering with other such communities and organizations in their exercise of the same rights. The Roman Catholic hierarchy is dead-set against women's reproductive rights. Its bishops and prelates have the absolute right to require their constituencies to eschew birth control and abortion on pain of excommunication just as elders of the Church of Jesus Christ of Latter-day Saints (LDS) may insist that members of their church abstain from alcohol and other substances, in the same way the Baptists demand adult believer baptism and ban infant baptism. But none of these churches must attempt to force nonbelievers to comply with their programs, and certainly not by lobbying Congress and state legislatures to make civil and criminal statutes out of church law. No American Shariah, thank you very much.

What churches, synagogues, mosques, and temples are perfectly free to do under the First Amendment is to compete with one another by vending their wares in the religious marketplace and rolling out the welcome mat for the curious inquirer. That's the approach most of the up-and-coming so-called mega-churches follow, and as anyone can see when the television cameras pan their vast auditoria, they are successful. It's generally a hard-sell proposition once you're inside, but there is no one to prevent your exit.

A secular humanist is perfectly content with such a situation and set of conditions. He or she is not required to answer the door when the Jehovah's Witnesses or the LDS missionaries come by. The humanist might wish that the real property of religious communities might be asked to share the tax burden, but he also knows that the proposition would never fly. It would become the subject of vicious demagoguery in Congress and legislatures, and no one entertaining hopes of being elected to any significant office would come near it.

The humanist is also insistent upon adherence to the body of law that has emanated over the last two centuries from the First Amendment prohibition of religious establishment. In particular, the humanist and his libertarian friends and neighbors will always resist the teaching of creationism or so-called intelligent design in public school science classrooms, not only because both notions fly in the face of known fact—for example, the Theory of Natural Selection and other well-documented hypotheses of evolutionary biology—but because they are essentially religious doctrines based on biblical texts.

Therefore, it may be said that the position occupied by religion in the republican democracy known as the United States of America is secure. The leaders of the several major faith groups sometimes wade inappropriately into politics to serve their own denominational ends or in efforts to secure one or another of their tenets in civil law. Others, though, speak out, often to their own disadvantage, for social justice and against unnecessary war and violence. Détente, if not entente, seems to be maintained, and that's probably the best America can do at this stage of its development.

Notes

1. An edited version of a public lecture given by the author on March 20, 2011, under the auspices of the Central United Methodist Church of Winona, MN, sponsored by Dr. William J. Richardson and Dr. Robin Devinney Richardson and their informal group of inquirers known as PiE.

2. Amos 5:24, ASV.

3. Rev. ed., Thomas Nelson, 2009.

Bibliography

Bailyn, Bernard. *To Begin the World Anew: The Genius and Ambiguities of the American Founders.* New York: Alfred A. Knopf, 2003.

Balmer, Randall. *The Making of Evangelicalism: From Revivalism to Politics and Beyond.* Waco, TX: Baylor University Press, 2010.

The Book of Common Prayer. New York: Oxford University Press, 1928.

The Book of Common Prayer. New York: Seabury Press, 1979.

Brooks, Andrée. "In Italian Dust, Signs of a Past Jewish Life." *The New York Times,* May 15, 2003.

Cohn-Sherbok, Dan, Harry T. Cook, and Marilyn Rowens. *A Life of Courage: Sherwin Wine and Humanistic Judaism.* Farmington Hills, MI: International Institute for Secular Humanistic Judaism, 2003.

Cook, Harry T. *Christianity Beyond Creeds.* Clawson, MI: Center for Rational Christianity, 1997.

_____. *Seven Sayings of Jesus: How One Man's Words Can Change Your World.* New York: Vantage Press, 2001.

Crossan, John Dominic. *The Historical Jesus: The Life of a Mediterranean Peasant.* New York: HarperSanFranciso, 1991.

_____. *Jesus: A Revolutionary Biography.* New York: HarperSanFranciso, 1994.

_____. *Who Killed Jesus? Exposing the Roots of Anti-Semitism in the Gospel Story of the Death of Jesus.* New York: Harper Collins, 1996.

Dawkins, Richard. *The God Delusion.* London: Bantam Press, 2006.

Dewey, Arthur J., Roy W. Hoover, Lane C. McGaughy, and Daryl D. Schmidt. *The Authentic Letters of Paul: A New Reading of Paul's Rhetoric and Meaning.* Salem, OR: Polebridge Press, 2010.

Doctorow, E.L. "Texts That Are Sacred, Texts That Are Not." Pp. 51–56 in *Reporting the Universe* by Richard Rorty. Cambridge, MA: Harvard University Press, 2003.

Donne, John. *Devotions.* Ann Arbor, MI: University of Michigan Press, 1959.

Ellul, Jacques. *Propaganda: The Formation of Men's Attitudes.* New York: Vintage Books, 1965.

Frykholm, Amy Johnson. *Rapture Culture: Left Behind in Evangelical America.* New York: Oxford University Press, 2007.

Guttenplan, D. D. *American Radical: The Life and Times of I. F. Stone.* New York: Farrar, Straus and Giroux, 2009.

Harris, Sam. *The End of Faith: Religion, Terror, and the Future of Reason.* New York: W. W. Norton & Co., 2004.

Hedges, Chris. *Death of the Liberal Class.* New York: Nation Books, 2010.

Jenkins, Philip. *The Next Christendom: The Coming of Global Christianity.* New York: Oxford University Press, 2002.

Larson, Edward J. *Summer for the Gods: The Scopes Trial and America's Continuing Debate Over Science and Religion.* New York: Basic Books, 1997.

Luther, Martin. "An Introduction to St. Paul's Letter to the Romans." *Vermischte Deutsche Schriften.* Vol. 63. Ed. Johann K. Irmischer. Frankfurt: Heyder and Zimmer, 1854.

_____. *Luther's Works.* Ed. Jaroslav Pelikan. St. Louis, MO: Concordia, 1956.

Marsden, George M. *Fundamentalism and American Culture.* 2nd ed. New York: Oxford University Press, 2006.

Nauta, Lodi. *In Defense of Common Sense.* Cambridge, MA: Harvard University Press, 2009.

Niebuhr, Reinhold. *The Irony of American History.* New York: Charles Scribner's Sons, 1952.

Pagels, Elaine. *Beyond Belief: The Secret Gospel of Thomas.* New York: Random House, 2003.
Pritchard, James B. *Ancient Near Eastern Texts.* Rev. ed. Princeton, NJ: Princeton University Press, 1969.
Roosevelt, Theodore. "The Puritan Spirit and the Regulation of Corporations." At the laying of the cornerstone of the Pilgrim Memorial Monument in Provincetown, Mass., August 20, 1907. http://www.theodore-roosevelt.com/images/research/txtspeeches/257.txt.
Rorty, Richard. *An Ethics for Today: Finding Common Ground Between Philosophy and Religion.* New York: Columbia University Press, 2011.
_____. *Contingency, Irony, and Solidarity.* New York: Cambridge University Press, 1989.
_____. *Achieving Our Country.* Cambridge, MA: Harvard University Press, 1998.
Wills, Garry. *Under God: Religion in America.* New York: Simon & Schuster, 1990.
Wine, Sherwin T. *Staying Sane in a Crazy World.* Farmington Hills, MI: Center for New Thinking, 1995.
Wood, Gordon S. *The Idea of America: Reflections on the Birth of the United States.* New York: The Penguin Press, 2011.
Wordsworth, William. "Lines Composed a Few Miles Above Tintern Abbey, On Revisiting the Banks of the Wye During the Tour," in *Nelson's English Readings.* Vol. 3. New York: Thomas Nelson and Sons, 1936.
Wright, Robert. *The Evolution of God.* New York: Little, Brown and Company, 2009.

Glossary

Agnostic: One who says he or she "doesn't know" whether or not another's proposition or proclamation is valid because there is insufficient data or knowledge to warrant acceptance; a religious agnostic is one who declines to affirm belief in a deity unless and until objective data can be produced to warrant such a belief.

Cynic: A term used by some New Testament scholars to account for Jesus and what they take to be the countercultural, anti-establishment utterances credited to him in his sayings included in the gospels of Thomas, Matthew and Luke.

Deist: One who believes in a first or primary cause, a power or force that set creation in motion and then withdrew to let happen whatever would happen—from the Latin *deus*—god.

Elohim: A Hebrew word that acquired the meaning of "gods."

Elohist: Pen name given the author/editor of a 750 BCE document that appears *passim* in the Pentateuch and other earlier Hebrew scriptures. The author/editor uses *elohim* when referring to the deity.

Hillel the Elder: A Jewish sage and scholar (c. 110 BCE–10 CE) associated with the composition of extra-biblical literature. He is widely credited with two sayings: "If I am not for myself, who will be for me? And when I am for myself, what am 'I'?" and "That which you hate, do not do to another. That is the entirety of the Torah; the remainder is the explanation; go and learn."

Humanist: One whose philosophy of religion is focused on the history, the potential, and the concerns of human being.

Logos: A Greek word that means "word," but in a larger sense of the utterance of power. "Uttering" is a word used in law to describe the writing of a check in place of cash, indicating buying power. See John 1:1–4 for the biblical locus classicus of the term.

Nebuchadrezzar: King of Babylonia 605–562 BCE.

Orthodoxy: Literally: "straight opinion"; in practice: theological propositions approved by dominant movements or hierarchies.

Pentateuch: Another name for the first five documents of the Tanakh (see entry below).

Secularist: One whose religion is concerned with the world as it is and can be, the here-and-now and its possibilities for good and ill; from the Latin *saeculum* meaning "the present world."

Shul: Yiddish term for "school"; in practice: temple, synagogue.

Tanakh: A name used in Judaic studies for the canon of the Hebrew Bible. It is an acronym composed from the first letters of the text's three divisions: Torah, Nevi'im (the prophets), and Ketuvim (the writings).

Theist: One who believes in a god that is both imminent and transcendent, that is intimately involved with the life of the universe, especially the human race on planet Earth, and that can be petitioned through the medium known as prayer to alter the natural order of things—from the Greek *theos*—god.

Torah: A Hebrew word for "law" from a root said to mean "to direct" or "point the way"; in practice the term refers to the first five documents of the Hebrew Bible, or the Tanakh.

Yahweh: An approximation of the Hebrew words for the English "y," "w" and "h." The vowel sounds have been supplied as approximations, so that the word is pronounced in English: ya-way. When the word appears in the Hebrew text it generally is translated "lord" but in the oral reading of Hebrew documents in the rites of Judaism in which speaking the "name" of God is forbidden, the word "Adonai," also meaning "lord," is used.

Yahwist: A pen name given to the author/editor of a 1000 BCE tradition that appears to have been compiled as late as 500–450 BCE. The author/editor used the *ywh* when referring to the deity.

Index

Al-Qaeda, 2
Altizer, Thomas, 97
Aquinas, Thomas, 72
Augustine, 5, 6

Bin-Laden, Osama, 104
Bright, Bill, 23
Bush, George H. W., 25
Bush, George W., 25, 80, 106

Carter, Jimmy, 22, 24
Clinton, Bill, 25
Clinton, Hillary, 25
Colafemmina, Cesare, 65, 72
Cold War, 86
Constantine the Great, 70–71, 122, 136
Coughlin, Msgr. Charles, ix
Coulter, Ann, 26
Cox, Harvey, 97, 103
Criswell, W. A., 22
Crossan, J. Dominic, 19, 58, 69, 73, 90

Dennett, Daniel, 7
Detroit, 143
Doctorow, E. L., 52, 56, 57, 59, 63
Donne, John, 109, 124

Falwell, Jerry, 23, 25
First Amendment, 75, 76, 83, 106, 152, 154, 157
First Vatican Council, 21
Frank, Anne, 115
Franklin, Benjamin, 122, 125
Friedman, Thomas, 122, 125

Garrett, W. Barry, 22
Gingrich, Newt, 154
Golding, William, 109
Gutenberg, Johannes, 55

Harris, Sam, 7
Hertsgaard, Mark, 139
Hitchens, Christopher, 7, 9

I Have A Dream speech, 62, 152
Irenaeus, 70–71

Jenkins, Philip, 106–7

King, Martin Luther Jr., 19, 24, 62, 115, 133, 144–45, 152
King, Rodney, 115–16
Kolton, Tamara, 129–30

Lessenberry, Jack, ix
Luther, Martin, 5, 7, 8, 9, 12, 19, 21, 24, 62, 72

Malcom X, 24

Nicaea and Council of, 71
Nixon, Richard, 24

O'Connor, Sandra Day, 25

Planned Parenthood, 142, 153

Rand, Ayn, 115
Ratizinger, Joseph, 26
Reagan, Ronald, 6, 24, 25, 106
Robertson, Pat, 23
Robinson, John A. T., 97
Roe v. Wade, 22, 76, 77
Rorty, Richard, 10, 12, 29, 52

Santayana, George, 10
Scopes, John, 23, 29, 46, 47
Stein, Herbert, 120–21

Taliban, 2
Tillich, Paul, 104–5
Trent, Council of, 21, 29

Vahanian, Gabriel, 103
Van Buren, Paul, 97, 103–5

Wine, Sherwin, 11–12, 18, 63, 130, 133
Wojtyla, Karl, 26

About the Author

Photo by George Waldman

Harry T. Cook is a graduate of Albion College, Albion, Michigan, and of Garrett-Evangelical Theological Seminary at Northwestern University with honors in Hebrew. He is the author of several books, including *Resonance: Biblical Texts Speaking to 21st Century Inquirers* (2011), *Christianity Beyond Creeds* (1997), *Sermons of a Devoted Heretic* (1999), *Seven Sayings of Jesus* (2001), *Findings: Exegetical Essays on the Gospel Lections* (2003), and *Asking: Inquirers in Conversation* (2010). He also wrote a biographical essay for *Life of Courage: Sherwin Wine and Humanistic Judaism* (2003). Recently retired after 42 years of active ministry in the Episcopal Church, he covered religion and wrote a weekly column on ethics and public policy for the Detroit Free Press in the 1980s and '90s.

www.ingramcontent.com/pod-product-compliance
Lightning Source LLC
Chambersburg PA
CBHW060526090426
42735CB00011B/2386